Start and Grow Your Faith-Based Nonprofit

Readers are invited to view and download a resource list that is supplementary to *Start and Grow Your Faith-Based Nonprofit.* The list links to sites that include examples of board job descriptions; nonprofit support networks; do-it-yourself tool kits for articles, bylaws, and annual reports; ideas for honoring volunteers; courses on grantwriting; federal grant opportunities; contact information for universities that offer doctorates in evaluation; and much, much, more.

The resource list is available FREE on-line.

If you would like to view, download, and print out an electronic copy of the resource, please visit www.josseybass.com/go/esau.

Thank you,

Jill C. Esau

COULD THIS BE YOU?

Janie Jones is a stay-at-home mom with two kids. Seven years ago, Janie felt called to help international students in her town who had little or no English skills. She began by inviting two students to her home for an hour of basic conversation. Within two months, she had fifty students and needed a larger meeting space. She contacted her church staff, who agreed to host the meetings once a week in the fellowship hall. Soon after that, fifty more students joined the group, so Janie needed helpers.

Janie asked some friends from church if they would come one evening per week to help teach foreign students English. The next week, twenty helpers showed up, and the group of one hundred students broke into smaller groups of five. The group continued to grow that first year until it outgrew the capacity of its new location. A local community college began referring its overflow English learners to the church program. The second year of the ESL class began in a larger room at the church and spawned an entire new church community conducting services in English and Korean. Immigrants found a sense of family, and multiple needs were met through a core group of willing servants.

This is just one example of what one person can achieve with a little vision and a lot of help. One wonders how many more people might be served with more resources. Could the group expand into other areas of service with more leadership? Would it benefit the group to form a new nonprofit corporation? How many other problems could be alleviated with the genuine concern and energy of regular folks like Janie and you and me? What other overwhelming social issues might be best tackled by bringing them down to the local level of care? And how do we make that happen?

What's your idea?

Start and Grow Your Faith-Based Nonprofit

ANSWERING YOUR CALL IN THE SERVICE OF OTHERS

Jill C. Esau

Foreword by
Stanley W. Carlson-Thies

Published by Jossey-Bass
A Wiley Imprint
989 Market Street, San Francisco, CA 94103-1741
www.josseybass.com

Library of Congress Cataloging-in-Publication Data

Esau, Jill (Jill C.), date.
Start and grow your faith-based nonprofit: answering your call in the service of others / Jill C. Esau; foreword by Stanley W. Carlson-Thies.—1st ed.
p. cm.
Includes index.
ISBN-13: 978-0-7879-7672-9 (alk. paper)
ISBN-10: 0-7879-7672-5 (alk. paper)
1. Nonprofit organizations—Management. 2. New business enterprises—Management. I. Title.
HD62.6.E858 2005
658.1'148—dc22

2005010919

Printed in the United States of America
FIRST EDITION
HB Printing 10 9 8 7 6 5 4 3 2 1

CONTENTS

FOREWORD

So you want to do something that will really help your hurting neighbors and neighborhoods? Maybe you've been inspired by President George W. Bush's call to "rally the armies of compassion." Maybe media reports or a trip into an unfamiliar part of your town has touched you deeply as you realize that as much as you might feel you are struggling, others nearby deal with much harder problems. Or maybe you listened—really listened this time—to the stories of families wrestling with poverty or addictions that were told in your church last Sunday by a visitor from a local service agency.

One way or another, you've heard a new call, a new claim on your wealth, talents, energy, and skills. Those aren't just needy people—they are your neighbors, and you will no longer walk past on the other side of the road. You are ready to go, to serve!

But just what should you actually do? How will you make the journey from answering the call to taking action so as to bring practical, effective, and sustained help to families in desperate straits? We all know it is true: good intentions don't automatically yield good results. And even a great plan remains inert, lifeless, unless people rally around and lend it their support. And even the best idea for a service program won't do much good unless it is undergirded by a solid organization.

Is this where you find yourself? Inspired but uncertain about how to actually move ahead? *This book is for you!* Jill Esau has been in your shoes, and she will walk with you through the steps you need to take to translate your call to serve into a program that will last and make a positive impact.

Of course, this isn't the only useful guide out there; Jill uses other resources and notes them for you, too. But this book is tailored just for you—the person of faith with a burning mission to serve neighbors but with little or no experience in social services. Jill will guide you from the very start, helping you sort out just what is in your heart to do, through the vital steps of defining and refining a plan of action, building an organization, finding support for the work, linking with others active in the same area of service, and evaluating what you do so that you can be sure your good intentions are yielding good results.

Thumb through the book and you'll see that Jill speaks to your concerns and hopes and beliefs as she guides you through these steps, explaining why each step is important and encouraging you to persevere through the tough work of meetings, paperwork, research, legal discussions, and personal visits to convince others to share your vision.

As you might know, the Faith-Based Initiative, which has been my area of service even years before it got the name, is dedicated to providing encouragement to and support for grassroots service groups. We understand well that such groups are often the closest and most trusted sources of help for "the least, the last, and the lost"—to use the phrase I heard often from John DiIulio, the first director and my boss at the White House Office of Faith-Based and Community Initiatives. Yet it is clear that many of these efforts, which were started and are sustained by people like you who answered the call to serve because they could not turn away, need to be strengthened. To do the most good, to be able to withstand challenges, and to win greater support, they often need a stronger organizational form, better plans, a solid board of directors, and a clear focus on evaluating outcomes. And when they look outward for support—for donations and volunteers from a corporation or a foundation grant or government funds—the potential supporters will want to know about the strength of the structure, the wisdom of the plans, and the documented outcomes of the work. And even when a grassroots group is content not to search for outside funding, these qualities are necessary so that the aspiration to help produces real assistance for the people who count on others to help.

So a book like this is a valuable contribution to the real work of the Faith-Based Initiative and the society-changing impact it is certain to have. For the Initiative—just like you—is committed to real service, a growing positive influence in distressed communities, and aid for individuals and families asking for help. No one who is serious about this political and social movement is in it merely to score partisan points or just to encourage service without care for outcomes or to secure more money for faith-based and grassroots groups regardless of whether they are doing good work. So, thank you, Jill, for converting your experience, training, and passion into such a useful, encouraging, and inspiring guide for people of faith just starting out on the walk of practical care for others!

One last note. If you have been inspired by a call to service and need guidance on how to translate your inspiration into actual deeds and a program of service, Jill wrote this book for you. But consider this possibility, too, as you read and pray through it: maybe your best contribution will be not to create another organization or another program but rather to offer your energy, passion, and resources to an existing program, perhaps something already started at your church or by a neighborhood group or even a secular service coalition. Maybe the people involved already have the right idea and just need the addition of your insight and volunteer hours. Maybe your best contribution is to guide them through the steps Jill explains in this book. Or if you are an accountant, lawyer, or banker, maybe your best contribution is your professional expertise: helping an existing group refine its budgeting and financial records or offering to guide faith-based groups through the incorporation process and to intercede when a government program denies them the chance to compete for grants or contracts. If you serve in some public office, perhaps your best service is not to start another group but to work with renewed insight for justice for all in the use of the community's social-service money, its zoning decisions, and its treatment of at-risk youth and returning prisoners.

One way or the other, I hope you receive this book as the gift that it is, from one believer with a heart of compassion to another—to you, a gift to help you answer your call to service with good works that make a real difference in the lives of needy neighbors and neighborhoods.

April 2005

Stanley W. Carlson-Thies
Director of Social Policy Studies
The Center for Public Justice

PREFACE

To say that this book was divinely inspired sounds silly and melodramatic in the twenty-first century. However, that is the best way to describe how it ended up in your hand today. Nor is it an exaggeration to say that it was written under duress or at least under conditions that any reasonable person would consider difficult. You see, I was actually held hostage by this book for over two years.

The first year, my captivity took the form of sleep deprivation. Four nights a week, on a fairly regular basis, I was awakened after a few hours of sleep with ideas, thoughts, and concepts swirling in my head, making it impossible to fall back to sleep. These thoughts were usually answers to questions I had been asked by ministry or community program leaders or just regular caring folks via e-mail or phone or through mutual friends regarding the Bush administration's Faith-Based and Community Initiative. My dreams, thoughts, and responses were so specific that I eventually learned that the only way to get back to sleep was to go to the computer and type them out and get them out of my head. This first year of nighttime inspiration developed into a fifty-page book proposal that I resisted writing for many months.

Isn't it precisely during such times of internal struggle that we often identify our true calling—our purpose in life? We come to the point of facing what we are truly passionate about or what we are particularly good at, yet we assume, sometimes for a lifetime, that we couldn't possibly take that new job or task or calling seriously. Too much risk could be involved. It might appear foolish to others whom we want to impress. Nevertheless, that nagging thought relentlessly awakens us night after night. It keeps us at the computer long after everyone else has gone to bed. We might even fantasize about acting on this persistent internal call by running some numbers or penciling out a business plan. But to take decisive action in the direction of that call, no—that would cost too much!

The second year of my captivity was the actual writing and editing of the manuscript that has become *Start and Grow Your Faith-Based Nonprofit,* which truly was an act of God. You see, once I accepted the fact that it was God who was calling me to write down the material included in this book, I still didn't accept the fact that the writing down would lead to an actual book! I only knew that I had to do what I was doing in order to get to sleep. As often happens with my rebellious nature, I tried to negotiate with God. I agreed to write down the things that awakened me and even organize them, over the course of a year, into a thorough book proposal, knowing full well that once the proposal had been submitted, I was "off the hook." Of course it would never result in a book. And besides, I didn't have time to write one.

I had a part-time job, a busy family including two teenagers and a professional husband, a dog, and way too many volunteer commitments. My mom had cancer, I had just completed a master's degree, and I needed to resume my workout schedule. Obviously, I wasn't the person for this job of writing a book on answering one's divine call. Surely a great many such resources were already in existence.

But every day, new people would phone or e-mail me desperate for information about how they could engage in or improve their social ministry. They were ordinary, stable, rational people experiencing, like me, sleepless nights and distracted thoughts about the direction in which they sensed God leading them. Each had a unique approach to solving a particular problem in his or her community. They just needed help to put their ideas into action. And no, there was nothing similar in bookstores. Eventually, I saw the handwriting on the wall and quit fighting the inevitable. I had to write down what I knew in order for others to be able to "answer their call." With this realization came a flood of tears, which confirmed that I, along with thousands of others, was answering my call in the process.

The drafting of the book proposal was long and grueling, but I was spurred on by the constant questions and phone calls from dedicated pastors and lay leaders who needed answers to their questions. The same few questions kept coming from all over the country. How could they participate in the Initiative? How could they expand their small but effective program to reach a broader constituent base? What other resources were out there that they didn't know about? At that time, very few people were informed on the topic of new faith-based and government partnerships. God spoke to me in my dreams and reminded me to do specific things that would help these folks. For example, I might need to call Pastor Bill tomorrow and connect him with Janie Jones so that he could learn how to start an ESL program in his church. These types of dreams kept recurring, convincing me that the Lord knew exactly what He was asking me to do and why!

One can only laugh about how this book became accepted by Jossey-Bass in San Francisco. The surest way I could think of to be released from my divine assignment was to submit the proposal to the most respected publisher in the nonprofit field. By submitting the proposal to Jossey-Bass, I would have satisfied my call to write the minimal amount of material and have it rejected by a reputable publisher. Oh, well, I figured, at least I had followed through on my call and could now resume a healthy pattern of sleep. After all, friends who had published told me in order to have my proposal accepted, I would have to send out an initial mailing of fifty copies to fifty different publishers and not to expect to hear any response for at least three months. Who had time for that? I just shot for the moon by sending one proposal, expecting to be rejected and hence relieved of all further obligations.

My one proposal was sent the day our family left for the Thanksgiving weekend. When we arrived home on Sunday night, there was an e-mail waiting from Jossey-Bass asking when we could talk about the proposal. I was excited and frustrated at the same time. How could this happen? God knew I didn't have time to sit down and write a book! Who would listen to me anyway? Could this mean I wasn't allowed to sleep yet? Could this mean that hundreds, perhaps thousands of people who were looking for answers and encouragement might find help through such a book? Was this really a serious divine assignment after all?

Within two months, I had a signed book contract with Jossey-Bass, the most prestigious publisher of nonprofit materials in the world. I had sent out one and only one proposal, never expecting it to be accepted. I have been assured from many sources, including my editors, that this situation never happens! How could that be anything but the hand of God?

I tell this story for several reasons: first, to remind each reader that every one of us has a divine call, whether we like it or not. Sometimes people spend a lifetime fighting against their call, their purpose, which leads to lack of sleep, unhappiness, despair, and even addiction. We are better off simply facing that call, even if it is on a step-by-step, day-by-day basis, hoping we don't have to travel too far down the path. Second, when we answer our call, God is faithful; He will complete the task in spite of our weakness and fear. He is eager to surprise us with joy and success in our work so that we can spread His love and joy to others. There is nothing we can't do through Him who gives us strength. Third, our call, if it is divine, is always much greater than what we think it is. We see through a glass darkly, with limited understanding. But our simple acts of faith and obedience are recorded in heaven for eternal glory. Why do we resist and drag our feet? Only what is done by faith will count in the end. Life is so short. Shouldn't we all get busy answering our call?

This experience has truly been a journey full of struggle and surprise. I'm ashamed that I doubted the Lord, but I'm thrilled that my attitude didn't affect the progress of the book. I feel humbled to be used in this way, and I hope to hear from readers how this book may have helped in serving more people in more productive ways. But as we go about answering our call, let us all remember not to touch the glory; the glory belongs to God.

Redmond, Washington Jill C. Esau
April 2005

ACKNOWLEDGMENTS

Just as I was held hostage by this book for two years, so were three other people: Greg, husband and father extraordinaire; Gretchen, daughter of the decade; and Spencer, model son of quiet strength. All three sacrificed for the cause without complaining once. Mom's occasional absence at dinner, sporting events, and weekend outings was a price they were all willing to pay so that this project could be completed and so honor God. I am very proud of each of them and pray that they, too, will seek, find, and answer their call.

Others who deserve special mention are Stanley Carlson-Thies and Stephen Lazarus from the Center for Public Justice. Their scholarly work promoting the Faith-Based and Community Initiative, not just in the District of Columbia but all over the country, is driven by the clear call each has received to serve the poor and oppressed. This book and many others would not have happened without Stanley and Stephen leading by example. Dave Donaldson, David Mills, and Kevin Monroe of We Care America gave me friendship, opportunities, and contacts that also helped form this text. Jim Towey, Jeremy White, Catherine, Jen, and everyone else at the White House Office of Faith-Based and Community Initiatives were extremely helpful and accommodating.

Other help and support came from Randy and Donna Storm, who provided a desert retreat for writing. Curtis Brown of BrandintheBox.com offered more ideas and energy than average. Russ Johnson and the Gestner-Johnson Foundation gave equipment and inspiration early in the process. Scott and Julie Spiewak of Fresh Impact shared publishing advice based on their many years in the New York book business. Debbie Walkowski, a dear friend and accomplished author, offered many tips for the book proposal; each improved the final product. Wilma Comenat arrived just in time to assist with final revisions. Johanna Vondeling, Allison Brunner, Dorothy Hearst, and everyone else at Jossey-Bass who took a chance with the early manuscript deserve huge thanks. Thank you also to my colleagues at World Vision and the hundreds of folks across our great nation who persistently asked questions and demanded answers that led to the final product you now hold in your hand.

Ultimate appreciation goes to the Lord for always completing the good work He begins in us, even when we resist and drag our feet.

—J.C.E.

THE AUTHOR

Jill C. Esau is the public sector grants manager for the Seattle/Tacoma Metro Division of World Vision, an international Christian relief and development organization. Her areas of focus include nonprofit leadership and management, grantwriting, developing church "side-door" ministries, fundraising and in-kind support, creative collaborations, planning facilitation, public policy advocacy, and program evaluation.

Esau began her career in ministry management in California after earning a bachelor of arts degree at the University of California, Berkeley, in 1980. She has worked in museum management, international art sales, Bible Study Fellowship, and public and private school leadership positions. She volunteers for the National Alliance Council for We Care America, serves as Washington's state representative for the Johns Hopkins University Center for Talented Youth, and is an adviser to the missions and youth programs at Timberlake Fellowship in Redmond, Washington.

Esau became interested in the Faith-Based and Community Initiative while earning her master's degree in nonprofit leadership at Seattle University's Institute for Public Service in 2001. Her thesis, titled "White Center: A Case for Collaboration," led to the advisory positions she holds in the Washington state legislature and the state's Department of Social and Health Services.

Esau and her husband, Greg, a lawyer, have been married for twenty-one years. They have two children, aged sixteen and fourteen.

INTRODUCTION

Pain exists. So does love. Successful social ministry is where pain and love intersect. It is nothing new; the struggle between pain and love is as old as human existence and will continue long after we're gone. The good news is that the struggle is not hopeless! My faith background, Christianity, gives us centuries of evidence that God intervenes on behalf of the poor and oppressed in the world through his willing servants. This same principle is found in every religious teaching through the ages. Some of us respond practically to His prompting because we can do nothing less.

If you picked up this book, you feel prompted to participate in this phenomenon. Perhaps you already know the joy and satisfaction of helping others who are without hope. Or maybe you have observed that satisfaction in those around you and want to experience it for yourself. You may also feel a nagging call to make the world better, but you can't seem to put your finger on what exactly you should do. Whatever the reason for your interest, the smallest level of effort you expend for the sake of one in need will, without question, bring you tremendous satisfaction. Why is that? The answer is simple: that is the way the human spirit is designed to work. It is the way we are wired by our Creator.

Yes, there are dark and terrible things in our world; but remember, good has overcome the bad in the form of loving sacrifice. That example is the fuel that empowers us to answer our perceived call. And lest we become overwhelmed by the enormous burden of that call, it's imperative that we remember whose call it is we are answering: it is God's call, God's work, and He will accomplish it as we cooperate with Him.

Today we see tremendous interest in social ministry due to the announcement of the Faith-Based and Community Initiative established by executive order of President George W. Bush in 2001. Though Congress has yet to approve or pass the president's preferred legislation into law, we do have historic support for faith-based social ministry–government partnership, going back to the earliest days of the Salvation Army, Catholic Community Services, and other relief organizations formed to catch individuals who had slipped through the cracks of society. We also have the 1964 Civil Rights Act, which protects religious organizations in hiring practices, and the 1996 Welfare Reform Act, which includes a series of provisions called Charitable Choice law.

Chapter Six outlines some specifics about the Initiative and suggests ways to pursue partnerships with government under the new guidelines. But it is important to mention up front that there is no special money now set aside for churches and faith-based social ministries. Opportunities have been expanded in several government agencies for these groups to apply for grants on an even footing with experienced and secular service providers. Each year, government purchases more and more services from the faith community. The process is complicated and often discouraging for novice applicants. This book is designed to help you navigate that process.

The material covered in this book is presented in a sequential order, assuming that you are ready to respond to the call or leading you sense. It takes a logical, systematic approach to moving an idea from concept to reality through the many requisite channels and the many obstacles that are sure to be encountered. If your organization is already established, you have more freedom to jump around and find the chapter that addresses particular elements of structure or operation pertinent to your existing programs. One sure sign of commitment to a cause is the willingness to seek out new or better ways to help others. Meeting the needs of others is the highest demonstration of the human spirit. Chapter One asks specific questions to help identify exactly what need you feel called to address. For every hurt we encounter each day, there are at least ten willing souls eager to jump into action to alleviate the situation. There are perhaps fifty different ways that any problem could be approached successfully. There are also several different resources that, if applied effectively, could leverage that success for multiple benefits. These principles are the foundation of the vast network of social ministry that originated in the church, with people living life following a path of faith.

For centuries, the group of individuals that has responded most effectively, most immediately, and most selflessly has gathered under the banner of faith. Faith that tells us that our present life is a prelude to an eternal one. And our present life is a testing ground on which our eternal life will be determined. Part of the test includes our response to the pain we see all around us. Part of the test also includes how closely we follow the example of some key figures in history. Just about every religion has several examples of selfless service. So then, this book will be beneficial not just to a single denomination but to people from all backgrounds and all walks of life who are called to serve in social ministry. *Social ministry* is a term used to describe any form of practical, tangible service offered in God's name on behalf of someone in need.

Each year, six hundred thousand prisoners are released into the neighborhoods of America. This year, more than one hundred thousand American teenagers will run away and choose to live on the street. In the years 2000–2002, some 8,378,000 men and women were unemployed in this, the most prosperous country in the world. Last year, 50 percent of Americans over the age of twelve admitted using controlled substances at least three times a week. After age twenty, the rate rises to 70 percent. In the confused and terrified state of the world today, who is minding the least, the last, and the lost?

Answer: The church is—just as it has for centuries.

But who is the church? Isn't it really just regular people like you and me? And every day, regular people just like us come up with creative ways to solve society's problems and then ask, "Now what do I do with this great idea?" How can regular folks package their ideas in a way that can move them from conceptual to actual, viable service to make a practical impact on people who are hurting?

Most people motivated to serve out of their core faith values have no related education, professional experience, or access to giants in the field. They simply want to help in their limited yet powerful way. They need to learn how to get started and keep the momentum going in order to achieve their personal goals of religious obedience or social contribution. But the vast majority of these people lack trust in "the system" and will only listen to someone who shares their path of faith. Left out of the loop for so long, millions of neighborhood servants exist in their own world, untouched by progress and technical advances in the secular realm. Even if initial finances are available, expertise is not. Too often, the end result is burnout.

An example is the Antioch Bible Church, which established a thriving addiction recovery program that grew to three sites around the region. It even had a state contract to provide substance abuse treatment. But without technical support and nonprofit management experience, the once effective director suffered burnout and abandoned the program. More than one hundred people were left without a safety net, and the church is reluctant to restart the program. With proper tools and instruction, a new director could have stepped in and saved the program.

The major contributor to program failure is lack of information and understanding. But it is impractical and unrealistic to expect these social entrepreneurs to enroll in a two- to three-year graduate program to learn management and best practices. Many examples exist of good projects that started off in a church or synagogue basement, helped a few folks in need, and languished for lack of proper planning.

Houses of worship are eager to support their enthusiastic, social-minded parishioners, but they too have little training in program development and related nonprofit matters. Usually the well-meaning church board will oversee the "side-door ministries" without actually knowing anything about them or the people they are serving. They probably don't need the graduate degree, but they need more than just a willing soul who cares in order to succeed. Many have never heard that establishing a separate 501(c)(3) corporation with a new board of directors can avert many problems.

The common thread running through each willing heart that has read this far is a passionate concern about a painful condition. This concern usually derives from personal experience, such as an abusive spouse, a relative trapped in addiction, or a wayward child. If this describes you, you have spent many nights crying out for answers and relief from the hurt. You have perhaps sought counseling and advice from wise friends and pastors. Finally, in your prayers, you have argued with that still, small voice inside that tells you, "You can do more than cry." As people of faith, we know that as we seek to serve the least among us, we actually serve the Lord. The paradoxical thing is that in that obedience, we discover some relief from our pain and true personal satisfaction.

Well, what do you do with all your concern and passion? Where can you turn with your energy and ideas? This book will direct you through that process. It will introduce you to proven practices in easy-to-follow steps so that you can immediately achieve effective service and avoid spinning your wheels. Chapter Two shows how to formulate organizational statements that will guide your decisions and strategies. Chapter Three introduces the many facets of nonprofit business and points the way to finding valuable help.

This book is written for all who have a heart to serve and a good idea to share. So whether your passion be child care, juvenile justice, health care, substance abuse, youth services, education, homelessness, nutrition, or something else, expect to be encouraged by what you read on these pages. The best ideas that bear fruit come from folks just like you—people who fight in the trenches of life everyday, who see what works and, equally important, what doesn't. Your ideas and your effort can change lives. Your ingenuity and your passion will motivate others to follow in your steps.

In the pages ahead, expect to find encouragement. Expect to be challenged. The information you'll glean will help you hone your ideas to a productive end. It will help you fill in the gaps on how to do what you believe you have been called to do. Expect to find new approaches to traditional service. Expect to be excited and also a bit overwhelmed. That is natural. It won't last.

Once you begin to make plans and raise money so that your plans can work—you'll read about that in Chapter Four—your confidence will grow. As that happens you'll be ready to think about taking the next step and setting up shop, as described in Chapter Five. This is not something to rush into no matter how well things seem to be going.

Take time to secure your position by forming partnerships, discussed in Chapter Six. Then you can increase public awareness for your ideas and activities by devising an advocacy plan, as laid out in Chapter Seven. These two steps will strengthen your resolve and confirm your call, as well as bring others on board to support your work. Believe it or not, your grassroots organization can influence public policy if you back your position up with authority.

Once you begin to implement the steps laid out in this book, you will see results. Chapter Eight teaches how and why you'll want to measure those results. And the Conclusion sums it all up. So whatever approach you take—reading each chapter in sequence or scanning through and selecting the topics that interest you most—keep a pencil handy as you read. Underline thoughts that trigger new ideas. Star things that you can use. Jot your notes in the margins so you don't forget. As you read, you will be inspired; you don't want to lose that inspiration on the following page, where you'll find even more practical advice.

It is my hope and my prayer that each of you will become strengthened and better prepared to follow your unique calling to serve others. In so doing, your life will be rich and fruitful and a precious contribution to the Kingdom of God.

chapter
ONE

Answering Your Call

How Do You Want to Make a Difference?

One of the hardest parts of attempting anything new is figuring out what you want to do and why. It's a lot easier to strike out in one direction and correct your course later if necessary. That's OK. But by answering a few simple questions at the start, a lot of aggravation can be avoided. So as you start this book, you will be asked to answer some very specific questions, such as "What is the exact need you feel called to address?" and "Who are you now, and what do you want your program to become?" and "How would you define the people you want to serve? Where are they, and how do they relate to you?" Then you'll assess your strengths, weaknesses, opportunities, and threats (SWOTs). All this assessment will set the stage for creating the wonderful program you envisioned when you picked up this book.

People with good ideas usually can't wait to jump in and get started. We visionary types can be our worst enemy for failing to plan well. Who would attempt to build a house without counting the cost? What person of faith would attempt to do anything significant without first engaging in some serious prayer? So give yourself every advantage for success. Gather some friends together and pray for specific direction and guidance over what you are about to attempt. Discipline your mind and heart to remain open to what you hear from God, no matter how impossible or disappointing that message might be.

Specific things to pray for include the following:

What exactly are you being led to do?

Who will work with you?

What is your timetable?

Where will resources come from?

Should you work full time or part time on this?

Remember, committing your process to prayer is not just a onetime deal. It is very easy to get off track if you forget to check yourself. Build a prayer team that will take the job seriously and remind you to consider carefully how you listen. Keep in mind whom you are ultimately serving. Don't forget to check every thought and idea against the answers you receive from your prayer sessions. Often what we *want* to happen is not God's best action.

Once you are "prayed up," you can begin the process of preliminary planning. The First Steps chart in Worksheet 1.1 is a simple, informal process that can be filled out in a couple of hours. These steps will give you handles for your ideas and structure for your planning. Later in Chapter Four, you will complete more thorough exercises, such as project planning, preliminary strategic planning, and logic model evaluation, which is discussed in Chapter Eight. But let's first flush out the basics so you know which freeway to jump on!

Remember, if you want to attract others to your solutions, you must acquire their confidence that you have thought through the details and counted the costs.

STEP 1: ASSESS THE NEED

The first step to take in pursuing your idea is to assess the need of the population you recognize needs help. This need assessment will drive everything you do. For without determining the need, working toward a solution is pointless. So sit down by yourself or with a group of like-minded friends who share your concern, and figure out what need you feel called to address. What inspired you with your vision to help? Perhaps it's a failing school in your neighborhood. Maybe it's your own children who can't get the level of education you desire, and private school isn't an option. Maybe there's a loved one in the depths of addiction; you recognize that the need for addiction counseling and addiction treatment services is far above the existing services in your area. Or you see a large number of single mothers with

Worksheet 1.1

First Steps: Initial Questions to Answer

1. What do I feel called to do?

2. Why do I feel urgency about this situation?

3. What is God telling me to do?

4. What difference will my action make?

5. What do I have that might help the situation?

6. Who do I know that will join me?

7. How much time, energy, and money am I willing to give?

dependent children living on the streets or in substandard conditions with no means of helping themselves. Whatever the situation, you must define the need so that you can build your strategy and focus your ideas to meet that need in a clear, logical, and effective way. Worksheet 1.2 can help.

Find evidence of the need in the media. Clip newspaper articles that mention the situation. Contact established services, and educate yourself about what is being done and what isn't being done to correct the problem. Build a file of pertinent information that will help you understand all the angles surrounding your concern. Look up statistics on the Internet. Research related government Web sites for data. Become an expert resource for other concerned folks.

STEP 2: DETERMINE YOUR PLACE IN THE PICTURE

Once you identify the need, the next step is to clarify your role in the process of meeting that need. Describe yourself and your relationship to the need. Describe your emotional attachment to the population in need and your prior experience or personal connection with respect to this situation. If you already have a committed group, describe the group's credentials and experience. List important associations you have developed.

Perhaps you feel called to mentor troubled youth that are adjudicated, incarcerated or who risk becoming incarcerated. You will want to describe any affiliation you have had with troubled youth. It may be that years ago your son found himself in trouble with the law. Having walked through that process for years, you have experience and authority in this realm, and consequently you have credibility in meeting a need.

This process will give you confidence in going forward with your idea. It will also convince others to assist you or invest in your ideas because you have walked a path that perhaps they have not. You have gained access to decision makers in a closed system that few have breached. You may have the ear of the "change agents."

STEP 3: LAY OUT YOUR SOLUTION

Now that you have assessed the need and figured out the role you want to play in the situation, you are ready to present your ideas and solutions. Your initial plan should be fairly narrow in scope so that you can maintain a reasonable expectation of success. Great ideas often fail because the vision is too broad and vague.

Worksheet 1.2
Need Assessment

1. What is bothering me in my community?

2. Why is it bothering me?

3. Who do I know that is suffering because of this situation?

4. What contributing factors are making the situation worse?

5. Who could do something about it?

6. Why does the problem persist?

7. How might God feel about this situation?

8. What might I do to help?

9. When will this problem get better?

10. Does anyone else feel the way I do?

In formulating your plan, answer these questions:

What do you think needs to be done?

What could help alleviate the problem you have identified?

What new approach are you proposing?

What action should stop because it is aggravating the situation?

What would be different if your ideas were implemented?

Try to keep your initial plan to four or five main activities. These should be written down and kept in a file. Using the example of juvenile justice counseling, you might want to propose gathering a few qualified volunteers to go to the local courthouse as juvenile advocates or to the justice center twice a week and invite kids to talk individually. Each session could last, say, thirty minutes or forty minutes or longer, whatever is appropriate. Describe how those conversations would evolve. What types of questions would you ask? What is your method for encouraging these kids? Would you use any type of literature or tools during your meetings? Lay out exactly what it is that you plan to do to meet this need.

Also think about where you will conduct your work. Identify the specific locations. Having precise demographic information is crucial in establishing your credibility. Is it realistic that your group of ten volunteers would be able to cover the juvenile justice system in the entire state—or the entire county, for that matter? Probably not in your infant stage. So determine where you plan to implement your ideas or program very specifically. For example, plan to start in the central county courthouse until your volunteer base grows. Or your volunteers might want to cover more territory, with each visiting a separate facility in the county, thereby establishing your program at ten locations throughout the county right away.

You might want to team up experienced advisers or lay counselors with inexperienced eager helpers, in which case you might have five locations in your startup phase. Plan carefully, and be very specific about where you will work.

STEP 4: SPECIFY THE PEOPLE YOU WILL SERVE

This is a critical step. Defining your target population will determine who will partner with you down the road. Will you zero in on a specific racial group? Will you work with boys and girls? Will you serve only young people between the ages of fourteen and eighteen? Or will you meet with any youths who are interested and willing to talk? Perhaps you will ask a judge to help make that decision. A judge's endorsement may help you gain access to more kids and resources quickly.

Often in America, minority communities are considered "high-need." That is not surprising; most social problems exist in "high-need populations" everywhere in the world. For example, some demographic groups experience high rates of substance abuse and school dropouts. These two behaviors are the major contributors to juvenile justice problems. By targeting these populations as one of your primary concerns, you could leverage your resources to serve several high-needs groups with identical methods.

How about the families of the kids you will serve? Do you intend to offer your expertise to help other family members address issues that may have contributed to the child's current problems? If so, your program may take on a more holistic feel. You may be able to garner support from various family support networks by expanding your scope beyond the child to the family. Are there younger siblings who show signs of following in the older sibling's behavior patterns? Should this issue be discussed with the family as a preventive measure?

Start-up organizations need to be mobile. Today, most start-up nonprofits begin in a home office. But if you truly want to be effective, you must to go to the heart of the need to prove your interest and concern and to gain credibility. So if you received donated office space in the best part of town but the need you want to meet is on the "other side of the tracks," decide how willing you are to travel to the area of need. If you fear for your life every time you enter a distressed neighborhood, then maybe this type of work isn't for you! Think specifically about how you will conduct your service.

Don't expect folks in high need to come to you. For many, busfare isn't in the budget. Later we'll explore the options of setting up shop in neighborhood churches and community centers. Remember, if you want to attract financial support, you must teach yourself and your team to think from the perspective of the people you want to serve. How likely is a single mother on welfare and living in transitional housing to hop across town to receive one hour of mentoring from some do-gooder in the suburbs? Not likely at all.

STEP 5: IDENTIFY YOUR STAKEHOLDERS

This step is a big reason why you want to take stock of your situation. After assessing the need you feel called to address, it is time to figure out who your stakeholders are. Stakeholders are any people that are affected by or affect the work you do (use Worksheet 1.3 to record who your stakeholders are; a sample stakeholder list is presented in Exhibit 1.1). Once you sift through all the people your work touches, you will be better equipped to provide the kind of care they truly need; you may also find that they can assist you in some way. Most funders want to know who you consider to be your stakeholders, so you are better off figuring that out right from the start.

Try to expand your reach in this exercise. Think beyond your daily interactions, which of course should be included on your list, but also include a level outside your immediate contact list. If you work with a local elementary school, you should also consider the middle school your stakeholder because the families you serve will one day end up there. If your church is your primary stakeholder, you should also include any alliance it is a part of because what you do could affect the alliance—and it may be able to help you, too!

Don't limit your stakeholder list to the population you serve. For example, if you have elected to serve incarcerated youth, think about how your services will touch the lives of their families, their parole officers, their fellow inmates, and the local law enforcement agencies. Include people and groups that your work affects even if they aren't aware of you. But be realistic and be able to back up your claims if asked to do so.

Keep in mind that your stakeholder list will change as you grow and attract more partners and donors. All will become part of your internal and external SWOT assessments.

STEP 6: CONDUCT SWOT ASSESSMENTS

Your final step, figuring out your strengths, weaknesses, opportunities, and threats (SWOTs), is an exercise that is best revisited each year because conditions change. It could take one hour or a full weekend, depending on how much you want to invest in it. This step will help you see where you and your ideas are in relationship to everything else around you. The purpose is to guide you in focusing your plans and to protect you from becoming, for example, the eighth Christian job training program within an eight-block area in eight months. (Use Worksheet 1.4 to work out your SWOTs; a sample SWOT assessment is presented in Exhibit 1.2.)

Worksheet 1.3
Stakeholder Identification List

Person or Group	Stake	Current Influence	Potential Influence	Potential Resources	Other Information

Exhibit 1.1
Sample Stakeholder List for Central Valley School, a Private Liberal Arts Institution

Person or Group	Stake	Current Influence	Potential Influence	Potential Resources	Other Information
Students	Education, future opportunities	Building reputation, community representatives	Requesting changes in curriculum or methods of learning	Future alumni, funding base, attracting other students to the school	Students have an unlimited and unpredictable impact on the school's future.
Parents	Investment, Children's Life Foundation	Extracurricular activities, fundraising, reputation, encouragement	Teaching methods, sports programs, new funding contacts, filling of staff positions	Board representation, community representatives, specialized teaching, assistance in difficulties	Many parents have expertise that could be helpful in specific school situations.
Extended families	Grandparents', aunts', and uncles' desire for kids' success	Financial gifts, attendance at events, emotional support	Greater funding, expertise	Business contacts, in-kind support, community representatives	Relatives could share information about how schools function in other cities and states.
Faculty and staff	Career, income, benefits	Spending six hours each day with students, administrative details, discipline, nurturing, inspiration to learn	Lifelong examples, role models, creation of memories and patterns for lifestyles, unlimited influence	Love, inspiration, guidance, stress and time management, future educational and career contacts	Relationships with teachers and staff are carried through life and can never be measured.
Board members	Investment of time, funds, and expertise	Direction for the school, fiscal responsibility	Future funding, future stability or instability of the school	New contacts, donors, in-kind support	The board can alter the profile of the school very quickly.

Food service providers	Meal preparation, hosting of events and meetings after hours and off campus	Friendly interactions with students, daily lunch planning	Modeling proper mealtime manners, clean-up procedures, and respect for others and school property	Teaching meal preparations and kitchen management skills, recipe preparation and presentation	This group could form a unit on domestic management as an elective course.
Neighbors	Maintaining a safe and wholesome area in which to live	Resistance to school construction, negative influence due to traffic	Support if invited to participate in functions	Volunteer help, parking allowances, community support, funding	Neighbors could cause difficulties if not handled properly.
City and county officials	Revenue generated by school permits and taxes	Final decisions on all facility matters	Forcible closing of the school if they decide not to reissue permits	Development of key relationships to help diffuse strife and ill will	Officials have tremendous power over the school and must be handled carefully.
State board of education	Curriculum and graduation standards, all aspects of education	Determination of what to teach students and when; requirements for testing and teacher qualifications	Right to change standards at any time, power to add or remove any aspect of instruction	Development of relationships that could warn the school of impending changes before a problem results	Even a private school like this one is at the mercy of this board; compliance is a must.
Volunteers	Investment of time, effort, and emotion	Freeing up time for staff and teachers, interactions with students	Doing work that would otherwise require payment	Friends with time to help, recess supervisors and other currently paid staff positions	Volunteers could provide many more hours of help if each brought a retired friend along.

Worksheet 1.4
SWOT Assessment

	Internal	External	Implications
Strengths			
Weaknesses			
Opportunities			
Threats			

Exhibit 1.2
Sample SWOT Assessment for Central Valley School, a Private Liberal Arts Institution

	Internal	External	Implications
Strengths	Quality of education, highly motivated and able students, committed families, new facility, high standard of discipline	Location, high value placed on education and challenge, positive image, professional expertise	DISCIPLINE: No time is wasted; more learning occurs at every level; students become leaders of tomorrow.
Weaknesses	Long-term funding, insufficient equipment, athletics program, low salaries, isolated population	Space limitations, negative public image, minimal presence in the community, newness of the institution, lack of government funding	FUNDING: Money concerns are fraught with insecurity about the future of programs, expansion, covering external costs, and attracting high-level faculty; they restrict opportunities for growth and cause daily budget stress.
Opportunities	Academic achievements, athletic achievements, strong sense of community, nurturance of leadership skills, untapped resources	Future leadership, increased enrollment and visibility, satellite campuses, invitations to lecture, ability to attract prestigious faculty, voucher laws	VISIBILITY: Visibility leads to greater opportunities for students after graduation, expands the funding base, and attracts faculty and students but could also invite criticism.

Exhibit 1.2

Sample SWOT Assessment for Central Valley School, a Private Liberal Arts Institution, Cont'd.

	Internal	External	Implications
Threats	Advances in technology, attitude of exclusivity, staff burnout, volunteer burnout, cost, student boredom	Public policy; neighborhood complaints; increased costs of utilities, permits, and association dues; negative public impressions, education laws	TECHNOLOGY: Even our motivated, disciplined, and highly able students could be stunted without the proper cutting-edge technology capabilities and training. This needs to be a priority.
Trends	The school's reputation is increasing due to student accomplishments. Parents are retiring at an earlier age to spend more time with their families. The school receives free expertise from professionals vested in its system.	The decline of public education contributes to many applications that can't be accommodated. Erosion of moral fiber and safety in public schools drives families to private options.	SAFETY: No institution is immune from social problems. Central Valley School must remain vigilant and aware of any instability or concerns of students and faculty to thwart a potentially dangerous situation.
	The administration is investing in development and community relations staff.	Higher income levels make private school tuition affordable to more families.	Decisions regarding expansion will need to be made.

	Families, students, and faculty are establishing stronger community bonds as a result of the new facility.	The population shift to semirural neighborhoods has brought many more families within commuting range of Central Valley School.	More weekend and evening events will be planned, which will in turn affect neighborhood traffic patterns.
	The school is now poised to extend itself into the greater network of private schools in the state.	Many families desire smaller classes for their children. Central Valley has a policy of sixteen per class, which attracts this type of parent.	School representatives will be asked to mentor other parent groups wishing to duplicate its model and success.
		Public policy is addressing the possibilities of charter schools and school vouchers.	Curriculum requirements could be affected.

The process is self-explanatory once you study the SWOTs form. The best preparation for this exercise is to pray for a creative, bird's-eye perspective on your work. Here are some hints you might use in filling out your SWOT chart.

Strengths

Do you have a good reputation in your community?

Do you know people in high places?

Are there impressive work-related results you can point to?

What kind of support do you already have?

These kinds of questions help you determine what your strengths are. Now come up with some of your own questions to ask your team.

Weaknesses

Do you lack funds?

Are you currently working out of a spare bedroom or the dining room?

Is there a lack of community awareness of your program?

Do you lack capacity to do all that you want to do?

It's important to be brutally honest here. Remember, you are doing an assessment—a self-evaluation. If you leave out important details, you'll find out about it later, when it's much harder to address.

Opportunities

Is there some other organization that is asking you for help?

Are there facilities available to you free of charge?

Is there a tremendous need that you can help meet?

Is there a partnership already formed that you can join?

Think of what might be available even if you haven't taken advantage of it yet.

Threats

What is hindering your work or has the potential to do so?

Are you in temporary facilities that may not be renewed?

Do you have a negative reputation among key decision makers?

Are other organizations planning to start a program like yours?

You need to be constantly looking around to see how the landscape is changing day by day. Don't assume that the status quo will remain constant. Anticipate changes around you, and you could be on the cutting edge of what the real needs in your community will become.

This will be one of the most valuable exercises you will perform for your pilot program or your well-established, well-funded, well-respected organization. SWOT analysis is a best practice that every leader, board member, manager, or professional volunteer needs to be familiar with. It should be done by individuals and then as a group, depending on your situation. It could be performed at an extended board meeting, staff meeting, volunteer meeting, or organizational retreat with the help of an outside consultant. It doesn't matter how, when, or where it is done—just do it! Do it early and do it often—at least once a year.

Well done! You have accomplished quite a lot by just following the steps laid out in this chapter. But now is not the time to pat yourself on the back. Now is the time to jump forward, while you are motivated and eager to learn more! Take all the information you have accumulated and compartmentalized and continue to refine it with the steps presented in Chapter Two.

chapter
TWO

Building Your Foundation

Mission, Vision, and Values

No organization can succeed without establishing clear-cut statements of its *mission, vision,* and *values.* In this chapter, I will walk you through the process of creating the core documents that will define what you do, for whom, and why. Use the worksheets provided, and give yourself plenty of time. In the end, you, your team, your supporters, and the people you serve will know exactly what your organization is all about. Future decisions will be easier and new partners will be drawn to you because you will have firm guidelines to chart your course.

Have you ever wondered how truly great companies become great? What is the difference between a mediocre business that doesn't grow and a Fortune 500 type? The same question can be asked about nonprofit businesses and to some extent social ministries. What has the Salvation Army done to arrive at a position of international reputation and respect? How did World Vision become one of the largest and most stable nonprofit organizations in the world in less than forty years? The answer can often be found in those three little words: *mission, vision,* and *values.*

Perhaps you're wondering, what could possibly be so important about three intangible concepts? Maybe you think you already have good guidelines for operations and just want to get on with the business of serving your chosen group in need. You may be right; then again, what could it hurt to imitate the model of thousands of successful businesses and organizations the world over? In fact, many organizations take this practice further and develop not only general organizational statements but departmental mission and vision statements as well. Some families have been known to compose family mission statements, and I even know individuals that take their work life so seriously as to write a personal mission statement that guides their daily decisions and priorities.

The real issue for faith-based organizations is *stewardship.* Good management—stewardship—is ultimately about caring for resources in the best possible way. It demonstrates the understanding that everything we have is a gift to be used in pursuing the most productive, most efficient, and most effective results. One way to accomplish this is to take all precautions to reduce waste. Your guiding statements are your first assurance of better management.

What if you have made the decision to operate your program under the auspices of your church or place of worship or other legal authority? Do you still need these guiding statements? If your church has a good mission statement and you report to that board of directors, isn't that enough? My experience says no. Although it may work for a while, eventually as your program expands you will need to have specific guiding principles to give it focus and definition to protect it from unrealistic demands of others or from spreading into territory it was never intended to serve. By drafting your own statements, you define your program's unique niche within the larger body and allow for the choice of later taking on a new role or not. But we all know what happens to those selfless saints who always say yes to everything: they burn out.

Just in case you are still skeptical about this concept, consider how you are going to keep yourself and your support network from "organizational drift," the most common and damaging malady of start-up and established social ministries. Entrepreneurial and creative people are often driven by the "tyranny of the urgent," or they have a pattern of choosing the immediate good while forfeiting a deferred better or best situation. Organizational drift is a condition that sneaks up on newer, less experienced groups regularly. It can show up as a new program that has little or nothing to do with the original intent of your founding planning team. For example, your HIV/AIDS hospice program may be running smoothly, and someone suggests opening a food bank under your same name and business structure. Usually the suggestion comes from a well-meaning friend or board member who might have heard from Pastor John that his local church wants to open a food bank. Good Pastor John has asked you to administer this project. Although it is admirable to collect and distribute food to the needy, such a venture could also derail your hospice service.

Derailing often results from attempting good projects at the wrong time or in the wrong place or with the wrong partners or in a direction that has little or nothing to do with your original call. Precious resources originally intended for your hospice program are suddenly redirected toward a project that diverts attention, energy, and volunteers from your specific call. Your statements will keep you on track and help you avoid counterproductive decisions such as this.

The antidote to organizational drift is solid binding documents that specify exactly what, why, how, and to whom your services will be directed. But guiding documents don't only avert disaster; they also help chart your course each step of the way. They tell in succinct language who you are, why you exist, what you do, and why. These statements build on your work in Chapter One. After you figure out the general ideas of what your organization will be and do, you must hash out your mission, vision, and values statements as insurance against your investment and stewardship over your time, energy, money, and relationships.

This process will take time, but it will be time well spent. You may accomplish the work in one afternoon, but experience has taught me that more effort will yield better results. A good way to attract leadership and identify truly committed helpers is to invite a select group to participate in this project. You may choose to devote a full Saturday, complete with food and some time for fellowship, before you jump into your work. Let folks know the start and finish time, who else will be in attendance, and exactly what needs to be accomplished. You may also let them know that this is the first of a short series of conversations in which you need their valuable input. This group could eventually form the core of a board of directors down the road.

Alert: I recommend that your group work together on these statements before you form your board. Differences in opinion, values, and purpose will emerge from this process, and someone you thought was your soul mate may turn out to have very divergent views. Your organization will benefit from the careful execution of sequential order at this juncture. Once a person has been invited onto your board, it is both difficult and awkward to later ask the person to leave. However, it may become necessary for the health and future of the organization. At any rate, your core group needs to be of one mind on issues of mission, vision, and values in order to succeed.

If all this information sounds overwhelming and you don't have the confidence to begin, you may want to find a consultant to help you launch the exercise.

Professional nonprofit consultants may be found through referrals or in Resource E at the back of this book. Cost varies, depending on the consultant's experience and clientele, but expect to pay between $50 and $150 per hour. You may also be able to find an acquaintance to perform this service pro bono (free), but make sure the person has successfully facilitated in this way before, or you may lose your core group due to impatience or incompetence. Alternatively, you may be able to find a charitable individual or foundation that believes in your cause and will underwrite the cost of such a consultant. We'll talk more about this in Chapter Four when we discuss fundraising.

VALUES

Start by asking, "What are our values?" Your values shape your individual and organizational belief systems. This is the best place to develop your spiritual foundation for your work. Outlining some core values will bring into focus what is important to you as you form your guiding statements. This step is crucial for faith-based groups because our actions are motivated by what we believe. "We behave as we behave because we believe what we believe," said Rosemary Jensen of BSF International. Secular organizations and for-profit businesses have their distinct values and motivations, such as particular social agendas or increased profits. But philosophical and spiritual values don't usually play a pivotal role in their corporate structures. So if the principle of defining your organizational values seems foreign to you, perhaps you are more familiar with secular business structures. (Refer to our Web site, www.josseybass.com/go/esau, for help with determining your values.)

You who understand that your role in life is to serve others out of love and concern will strengthen your conviction by identifying the specific values on which you base that service. These values then become the foundation for your mission and vision statements. Here are some sample questions to ask individually or collectively (if you are not working alone, substitute *we* for *I*):

1. What do I love?
2. What is important to me?
3. How do I want others to view me?

4. What has God taught me?
5. What do I want to show others about God?
6. How do I want to be remembered?
7. Where do I want to invest my time, talent, and resources?
8. How do I define success?
9. What is it I'm called to do with my life?
10. What does God require of me?

There are many other great questions that you and your team could ask. Add your own questions, and answer them as succinctly as possible. The answers will form the outline of your mission and vision statements. Use Worksheet 2.1 to get your thoughts flowing. (Some sample answers are presented in Exhibit 2.1.)

This is an exercise that allows you to boil down what you believe in a way that accomplishes something. It's the first step in developing the method you will use to tackle your goals, which will be further developed in Chapters Four and Eight.

After you have a good list of values, or value phrases, write down the three or four most significant ones through a process of elimination. Come up with a one-sentence values statement that you can incorporate into your mission and vision statements. It could read something like this: "I value God's sacrifice for us, His provision and sustenance, and the commission He placed on our lives to care for widows and orphans."

Picture a new house under construction. A values statement acts as the foundation for your work. You need to dig down and find your core concepts upon which the rest of your work may be built. Your mission statement acts as the structure and arrangement for your work—the walls and rooms that divide and organize your activities in a way the allows you to effectively implement many projects, as well as a roof that puts limits on your grand dreams. Your vision statement is the ideal picture you hope to see when you stand across the street and view the whole image, with paint and landscaping and other details. Your vision is what attracts others to come inside and take a look or sit down for a refreshment and some deep dialogue. It becomes an asset to the entire neighborhood.

Once you have some personal and organizational values articulated, you are ready to attempt your mission statement.

Worksheet 2.1
Values Worksheet

1. What do I love?

2. What is important to me?

3. How do I want others to view me?

4. What has God taught me?

5. What do I want to show others about God?

6. How do I want to be remembered?

7. Where do I want to invest my time, talent, and resources?

8. How do I define success?

9. What is it I'm called to do with my life?

Add your own questions:

10.

11.

Exhibit 2.1
Sample Answers to the Values Questions

1. What do I love?

   Mercy, forgiveness, salvation, devotion to God, honesty, restoration . . .

2. What is important to me?

   Binding up the brokenhearted; caring for widows and orphans, leading the lost to the truth . . .

3. How do I want others to view me?

   As steadfast, long-suffering, faithful, committed to the truth, self-sacrificing, motivated by love, a healer of the sick . . .

4. What has God taught me?

   How to put others first, how much He loves us, how much He loves those who don't know Him; that time is short, the harvest is ripe, and the workers are few . . .

5. What do I want to show others about God?

   That God is all-knowing, all-loving, eternal, a provider, a lifter of hearts, the creator and sustainer of life . . .

6. How do I want to be remembered?

   As a servant, a trailblazer, an advocate, a coworker, someone who never grows weary of doing good . . .

7. Where do I want to invest my time, talent, and resources?

   In education, in building the Kingdom, in reducing abortion, in teaching others how to worship . . .

8. How do I define success?

   By serving urban families in the cycle of poverty

9. What is it I'm called to do with my life?

   To love God with all my heart, soul, and mind and to love others as I love myself

MISSION STATEMENT

Recall that this process may take a few meetings to complete, or you could work through it in a day. The important thing is not to become so frustrated that you settle for anything less than what you really want. It's OK if you need to take a break and finish only a portion of the work at one meeting. This is a creative work, and producing a high-quality statement requires a lot of prayer, undistracted attention, and positive attitudes. Keep the session productive so that you don't lose the interest of your team. It is essential that you produce something tangible in each session in order to keep everyone engaged and committed. You may want to designate two or three people to do the first draft; then bring it to the larger group to confirm the draft or to edit it. This approach protects everyone's time and keeps group members feeling positive about their participation.

Worksheet 2.2 will help you get the ball rolling when writing your mission document. Notice how simple the questions are. Resist the temptation to oversimplify this task, however. You'll return to the job repeatedly if you don't take it seriously at the start.

Some experts say that an effective mission statement should be no longer than twenty words. Some say it should be a full paragraph. Some believe it should say everything your organization does; others recommend leaving some room for alterations and expansion. The bottom line is that you are the expert on your organization. You decide what your statement should include and what it should not. Feel free to blend in some language from your earlier values work if you don't want to have a separate values statement.

So ultimately, you should end up with a statement that reads something like this:

> The God Loves You Shelter exists to provide temporary housing for homeless youth and to convey God's love through mentoring, tutoring, health care, and nutrition in Denver's central district.

This fairly general statement leaves room for partnerships and added services through the definition of *mentoring.*

Another more specific statement reads:

> The Crisis Pregnancy Center serves girls in the urban center of Dallas with medical care, pregnancy testing, adoption information, and family counseling, all in an effort to reduce the number of abortions in Texas.

Worksheet 2.2
Drafting Your Mission Statement

1. What is our organizational purpose?

2. Whom do we serve?

3. To whom do we direct our activities?

4. Why do we do our work?

5. Where do we do our work (generally)?

6. With whom will we partner?

Once you have your written mission statement, you should print it and post it everywhere. You should require that your staff, board, and volunteers all memorize it. Reprinting materials each time you change your statement can be expensive and frustrating. Try to come very close to expressing it perfectly the first time so you don't have to revisit the issue six months later.

Some mission statements, as in large public universities, have an opening statement and then subsequent paragraphs telling about the many different departments under the larger university umbrella. These types of statements often run to many pages and can be tedious to read through.

Avoid being too nitpicky when drafting your first mission statement. Rather than argue over the placement of punctuation, which does happen, defer to a grammar expert who can solve that question easily without causing undue hostility. Also, if you are starting out under the authority of a larger organization, such as a church, it's a good idea to have a representative from the church board or staff present when drafting your mission statement because your statement should tie you to your parent organization in some way. As you begin fundraising, potential funders will want to see firm accountability and agreement between you and your host or parent entity. Including similar words or phrases in your program mission statement will make it obvious that you are working in concert with your fiscal or parent agency, which strengthens your credibility.

You've written a succinct and satisfactory mission statement? Congratulations on completing a very important step in forming or expanding your faith-based nonprofit! From now on, when you feel like you've lost your rudder or direction, simply refer to your mission statement and you should realign quite easily. Questions like "Should we help organize the citywide Walk for the Cure?" can be matched against "What is the mission of our organization?"

DRAFTING YOUR VISION STATEMENT

Many experts think the vision statement is a waste of time and energy. They feel that such statements are too unrealistic to be of any use. That may be true for some. But if it's used properly, a vision statement can serve in a guiding role. Like the values statement and the mission statement, the vision statement puts into words the emotional reasons why we feel called to do what we do.

The mission statement tells what you do, for whom, where, and how. The vision statement tells what overall effect you hope to have by doing all that stuff. It answers such questions as "What is our preferred future?" "What is the ultimate goal of our activity?" and "How will the world be different as a result of what we do?"

Drafting your vision statement gives you an opportunity to state publicly what your dreams for the world are. If that seems unnecessary and frivolous to you and your team, don't write one. But I think it helps direct your decisions along a consistent path. It is also reassuring to your partners and investors to know that you aren't working on a means without a defined end. Your vision is the end to which you are continually working.

So looking back on all your preliminary work from the values and mission statements, formulate a concise preferred vision for your program or organization. Worksheet 2.3 should provide some help.

PUTTING IT ALL TOGETHER

Now what do you do with these statements? First of all, you must memorize them. Everyone in a leadership position in your program should be able to recite at least the mission statement from memory at a moment's notice. Why is that important? Remember why you are doing this: it is because you value *X, Y,* and *Z.* You are not engaged in this work for your own benefit or on a whim. You are called to this work by God, aren't you? So you need to be absolutely convinced of what you are doing and why you are doing it. You will not be convinced, nor will you convince anyone else to help, if you can't clearly state what the purpose of your work is without confusion.

Some people refer to this as the elevator test: if you can recite the mission statement of your organization to strangers in an elevator and leave them wanting to know more, you have passed the elevator test. You have proved yourself knowledgeable and articulate in what you believe and do, and you have successfully raised awareness where there was none. This practice is not only encouraging to you but is an effective marketing tool as well.

Exhibit 2.2 presents a generic sample of a combined statement for a social ministry. As I mentioned early on in this chapter, your statements are not chiseled in marble. You should reevaluate them at least once a year to make sure everyone still believes what was agreed to during the original drafting period. Just remember that it can be expensive to reprint all the materials on which your mission statement appears, and it can be confusing for volunteers and staff if your statements change dramatically. So give careful attention and consideration to adopting and fine-tuning your statements.

Worksheet 2.3
Drafting Your Vision Statement

1. What would your perfect world look like?

2. Why do you imagine a perfect world looking like you described?

3. What can your organization or personal effort contribute to your perfect world?

4. How much of your work is driven by your desire for your perfect world?

5. What are the obstacles preventing your perfect world from becoming reality?

6. Who shares your vision?

7. How can you motivate others to catch your vision?

Exhibit 2.2
Mission, Vision, and Value Statements for a Social Ministry

Mission Statement

WCNW exists to support faith-based and community-based nonprofits with partnerships, resources, advocacy, and capacity building for increased effectiveness and expanded services to the poor while promoting self-sufficiency.

Vision Statement

WCNW envisions healthy self-sufficient families whose physical, emotional, and spiritual needs are met by reputable and unified faith-based nonprofits guided by Christian principles that lead dependent people toward economic independence.

Values Statement

We value relationships with Christ that build up the church and its partners. We value prayer and creative approaches to addressing the needs of the poor. We value unity and combined effort when it results in tangible, repeatable outcomes, and we value accountability, which ensures that we accomplish our goal of meeting the needs of the vulnerable among us.

By now, your team should be feeling pretty good about all you have accomplished. Just for fun, take an unscientific poll of how each team member now perceives the future of your organization. Ask a few simple questions, such as these:

"How well did you understand what we were trying to do before reading Chapters One and Two of *Start and Grow Your Faith-Based Nonprofit*?"

"How well do you think you understand what we are all about now?"

"Do you feel ready and equipped to take the next steps toward realizing our organizational goals?"

Don't be disappointed if some team members still feel uncertain. That is completely normal and provides a cautious approach for what comes next.

You now have the momentum to move into the next phase of your call: electing a board to guide your work and to consider business and budget issues to frame it all.

chapter
THREE

The Nuts and Bolts of Your Nonprofit

Incorporation, Boards, Budgets, and More

Now is the time to think about your business procedures and protections. You know what you do and why. You know how to describe your ministry in concrete terms that others can grasp. Let's make sure you can also function within the limits and boundaries of the law, minimizing the risk of legal problems before you really get off the ground. This chapter will show you how to develop a board of directors for maximum effectiveness and find professional services at minimal cost. We'll talk about incorporation, accounting needs, volunteer management, and budgets. None of these activities are as much fun as the ones in Chapters One and Two, but they don't have to be all drudgery either.

The business aspect of social ministry is the driest part of your work. However, it is also one of the most important parts. This chapter is intended to be a brief introduction to the technical management issues your program will face. It is not and cannot substitute for legal advice because (1) I am not a lawyer or a legal expert and (2) not only are these issues complicated but also changes occur that are hard to keep up with. So you should regard this information as a thumbnail sketch of what is involved in starting and maintaining a 501(c)(3) nonprofit organization (known by its IRS code number). We'll not take the time to discuss the other types of 501(c) organizations (there are twenty different tax-exempt categories) because they are not likely pursuits for the audience of this book (but if you are interested, you may visit www.irs.gov/charities/topic/index.html for an extensive list of tax-related issues and answers). The 501(c)(3) status refers to any organization formed to provide religious, charitable, scientific, public safety, literary, or educational services or to prevent cruelty to children or animals. Your organization probably falls into one of these categories. Stick to the guidelines for tax-exempt status, and you should have no problems. But realize that highly experienced and reputable people and programs have run into problems that you should learn from.

You could develop the best program in the world in terms of effectiveness and life impact, but if you don't manage the business details properly, you could end up losing your legal status. I don't say this to frighten you, but the matter of management is that serious. Years ago, an organization may have been able to fudge on insurance issues or bylaws compliance. That was before the well-publicized non-profit scandals of the 1980s and 1990s, involving the misappropriation of funds by televangelists, the Red Cross, and private foundations. Since then, federal and state oversight agencies have been cracking down.

Perhaps you are thinking, "How can that be? How could good people who want to help others become involved in scandals?" The answer is as old as the Garden of Eden. Even well-intentioned, loving people have an imperfect human nature. None of us is free from the temptations of greed, overcommitment, sloth, procrastination, and so on. This is why accountability is so critical to the structure of your work. In the nonprofit realm, we have layers of accountability: to government regulations, donors and funders, investors, boards of directors, stakeholders and partners, and also our constituents, the people to whom our services are directed. One would think that these would more than safeguard our operations from impropriety. But Murphy's Law is alive and well, even in charitable institutions: if something can go wrong, it probably will. Thank goodness we have committed saints who willingly serve on charitable boards!

Not so long ago, the duty of caring for the sick, indigent, widowed, orphaned, uneducated, and general needy population fell to the church. Over time, governments have picked up more and more of the responsibility but continue to recognize the enormous contribution congregations and houses of worship have made to society. Ever since the founding of our country, special exemptions from taxes have been applied to religious organizations. In fact, it is widely conceded that if churches and parachurch organizations should one day stop performing social ministries, it would be impossible for the government or any other entity to meet the needs in the United States alone, not to mention the rest of the world.

THE GOVERNANCE OF NONPROFITS

How are churches, social ministries, and other nonprofit organizations managed and governed? Each has a volunteer board, usually consisting of a combination of elected and appointed members, that shapes policies and procedures; appoints or hires a manager, such as an executive director; approves budgets; guarantees bylaws compliance; and shoulders the myriad other responsibilities of running a business. A church may have a board of deacons or board of elders. Other nonprofits usually have a board of directors to lead and guide the organization. The big difference between nonprofit organizations and businesses is the distribution of profits and income. A large for-profit company generally has stockholders that receive dividends out of the company's earned profits. Nonprofit organizations are not operated so as to earn profits; they receive donations, grants, or small amounts of earned income from fees for services, which go right back into the organizational or program budget to cover the cost of additional services and programs. Staff are paid on an hourly, salary, or contract basis.

DECIDING TO MOVE FORWARD

If you have decided to go forward with the incorporation process, you will save yourself and your organization a lot of grief by doing some research, engaging professionals such as lawyers and accountants, and putting your business affairs in order right from the start. However, this may be the time to ask yourself and your team, is forming a new nonprofit organization the best way to go?

Most motivated social entrepreneurs have spent a significant amount of time volunteering or helping out in their field of interest before they reach the point of heeding the call to serve in a leadership position. Many of you have become experts in your field by virtue of the time, talent, and resources you have invested in a social ministry or church program. Now you see a better way to do things; you know that there are many more folks in need who could be helped by your service if a few minor changes could be made. You have mentioned your ideas to the program leaders, but they have other priorities and can't or won't implement your ideas. So you assume that the only way to proceed is by starting your own independent organization where you can do the same or similar work using new methods and achieve greater results. You may be right; then again, you may defeat your entire purpose for serving. The reason is that *reinventing the wheel is rarely cost-effective.*

Remember the principle of counting the cost? After reading this far, are you surprised at the amount of work involved in starting "your own" organization? Every year, thousands of nonprofits cease operations for a multitude of reasons, but the most common is a lack of funding and capacity to meet the demands. Unless you can exceed the performance of an existing program that does the same type of work in every area including fundraising, it is unrealistic to think that you can do better on your own. We'll talk more about this in Chapter Six when we discuss partnership. At the risk of discouraging you from finishing this book, I urge you to think realistically about the true cost of going out on your own. Make sure you aren't suffering from the "greener grass syndrome."

A good question to ask is, "Have I exhausted all possibilities for making this project work the way I think it should within its current framework and under its current governing body?" If the answer is a strong yes and you are "prayed up" on the matter, then it could be the right time to move ahead independently.

Don't assume, however, that forming a separate 501(c)(3) organization is the only way to go. What might make more sense for you and your ideas in the early stages is to approach another tax-exempt or parent organization (church, larger social ministry, established parachurch organization) and present your ideas with the understanding that if you establish a partnership arrangement, you will retain control of day-to-day operations while functioning under the parent organization's authority. It is important to understand that no matter where you end up with your program, you will still need to come under the governance of a board of directors. So let's talk about that.

THE BALANCE OF POWER

If you are a service practitioner—that is, if you are the worker bee who has direct contact with clients (also known as constituents, people in need, folks you serve, or your target population)—chances are that you have a tendency to become impatient with paperwork, frustrated in meetings, and prone to exclamations such as "Just leave me alone and let me do my work!" You probably have no interest in parliamentary procedures and don't care that Henry Robert, who first compiled his *Rules of Order* in 1876, still dictates the standards for conducting meetings today. Consequently, you and others like you may breathe easier because of the governing board concept.

Your board of directors is the body that watches your back as you practitioners go about saving the world. They are volunteers who share your vision and want to use their own gifts and talents to answer their call. They also have the role of supervisor or boss in a nonprofit organization. In a start-up or young organization, the board approves all expenditures, hires the manager or executive director, or even acts collectively as the executive director for a limited time. The board is the governing authority that holds all risk and liability and maintains financial accountability for the organization or program. It's a brilliant checks-and-balances system that has worked well for centuries.

A TYPICAL SCENARIO

You have decided it's time to take the next step in your call to ministry. You gather a few friends of like mind and pray about what to do next. You find a few resources, like this book, and eventually decide to form your new nonprofit organization. You discover that the first step is to assemble your leadership, or board of directors, so you and your core group of friends establish your board and elect one another as officers: president or chair, vice chair, secretary, and treasurer. Now you can at least get off the ground and start the process of obtaining tax-exempt status and raising funds. This is how 90 percent of all nonprofit organizations get started.

There is nothing wrong with this scenario—it has worked for millions of people for decades. But remember that thousands of nonprofits cease operations every year. Leadership and board profile have a lot to do with that failure rate. Might there be a better way to set up your corporation? Might you save some time and aggravation by thinking this through a bit differently, a bit more long-term?

Consider what is at stake in the governing body of your future organization. These folks will make all the major decisions for your program. They will have the power to move you forward or hold you back. They'll represent you out in the community, for better or worse. And they will not only hold the purse strings, but they should also help fill the purse! All that being said, don't you want to think your board profile through a little more thoroughly?

RECOMMENDATIONS FOR BOARD FORMATION

I propose that you take five explicit steps in the process of assembling your nonprofit board.

Step 1: Investigate

Identify other nonprofits that you admire, and interview key staff or board members (or both). Ask lots of questions like these:

> "If you had it to do over again, what would you do differently in setting up your board?"
>
> "What does your board do well, and what does it struggle with?"
>
> "What is your board policy on personal giving and fundraising?"

Ask good questions of these people, and you will get lots of good and different answers—answers that will help you make decisions about your own organization. This doesn't have to be a formal process; in fact, it's better if it's not. Just invite these folks to sit down over coffee for an hour and "pick their brains." They might end up referring you to good potential board members.

Don't worry about being rejected in this. Service-oriented leaders love to be recognized for their effort. You will be honoring them by acknowledging their expertise. Simply explain that you respect the work they do and are eager to learn from "the best." This step could also lead to a great partnership down the road.

As in all relationships, be respectful, humble, and supportive. Guard against appearing like the white knight on horseback who has trotted in to take charge of a desperate situation. We'll discuss the delicate reality of nonprofit relationships in Chapter Six.

Step 2: Create a Board Profile Grid

The distribution of duties is very important on your board. Avoid appointing board members who are all alike. The profile grid in Exhibit 3.1 gives you some points to consider; you may need to add other qualifications to fit your situation. Balance is the second most desirable goal for your board. Don't lose sight of the primary goal of your board profile: unity of vision.

Look back at Chapter Two for a refresher on organizational vision. If there are divergent visions on your board, you will never have complete commitment from anyone. Divergent visions reflect uncertainty, lack of focus and direction, and

Exhibit 3.1
Profile Grid

Position	Name	Professional Affiliation	Board Experience	Community Contacts	Giving History	Invited by
Chair	Bill Poe	IBM Manager	Church	Numerous	Extensive	Joan Lies
Vice chair	Kay Long	U.S. Bank	United Way	Central District	Short-term	Al Moyer
Secretary	Pete Hughes	Lake City Church	Elder board	Mainly churches	Yes	Pastor Smith
Treasurer	Sue Mills	KPLM	None	Some—accounting firms	Not much	Past chair
Director 1	John Ekes	Attorney	Boys & Girls Club	Many–legal	Unknown	Judge Roy
Director 2	Jeff Jones	Pastor	20 years	Numerous	Yes	Bill Poe
Director 3	Guy Cast	Graduate student	Student union	University campus	None	Past secretary
Director 4	Mary Hall	Missionary	SIM International	Church community	Yes	Rev. Stone

limited chances for success. Remember, your mission may be fulfilled in various ways and through various means, but your vision remains consistent—it represents what you are ultimately striving to accomplish. Vision agreement must be the first and foremost qualification of any board member.

Step 3: Draft Board Job Descriptions and a Code of Ethics

An example of a board job description is presented in Exhibit 3.2. Exhibit 3.3 features a code of ethics for board and staff members, an added protection that many organizations are now adopting. You can find more examples and links to excellent nonprofit board support networks on our Web site at www.josseybass.com/go/esau. Preparing these forms may seem tedious, but they are lifesavers later on when you need to clarify who does what. They also help potential board members understand exactly what is expected of them if they agree to serve, and they show that your leadership core has its act together by bothering to set these crucial details in place before inviting people to serve. Notice that the term of service is indicated on the job description. That is one of the most important decisions you will make. One of the first questions people will ask is, "How long is the term?" Anticipate those questions and be ready with answers. Doing so will convince your potential board member that you won't waste his or her valuable time.

Step 4: Make a List of Potential Board Members

The list of potential board members has probably been forming in your mind for a long time. These individuals are people who cross your path in the course of each day as you go to church, do volunteer activities, and attend political events, school functions, and fitness classes at the health club. Your short list will most likely include high-profile people who have demonstrated commitment to your cause at least as long as you have.

Note that your board will get off to a healthy start if you have a few experienced, mature members from the beginning. Avoid stacking your board with inexperienced buddies from Bible study or aerobics class. If you are serious about this new organization (and you'd better be to be going through all this work!), you'll want to give yourself every advantage for success by bringing on experienced, proven board members who know the ropes of organizational leadership and have served on high-powered boards in the past. This is, of course, easier said than done!

High-powered board members are aggressively sought by—no surprise—high-powered boards. So chances are that they are overcommitted already. How

Exhibit 3.2
Duties of Board Members

Members of the ABC Shelter Board of Directors are expected to support and promote the following duties during their term of office:

1. Determine, promote, and defend the organization's mission, vision, and values.
2. Hire and oversee executive staff within the management structure and guidelines.
3. Serve as support and coach for executive staff through regularly scheduled meetings and conduct annual reviews.
4. Conduct planning and budgeting processes that guide program and departmental decisions.
5. Attend 80 percent of all board meetings and serve on a committee.
6. Manage resources responsibly as stewards of trust.
7. Monitor program growth or decline and service expansion and partnerships.
8. Commit to making a personal contribution and to developing new sources of revenue and financial support for the organization.
9. Identify new members as assets for future board membership.
10. Provide opportunities for public awareness and visibility for the organization, thus serving as advocate and spokesperson in the public square.
11. Participate in an evaluation of the board's effectiveness and performance annually.

____________________ ____________________

Name of Member | Date and Term of Office

Exhibit 3.3
Code of Ethics for Board and Staff

Purpose: The purpose of this Code of Ethics is to ensure the highest level of conduct and management over the affairs of the XYZ Food Bank. All staff, volunteers, and board members are expected to sign this statement at the time of participation.

Code: Upon associating with the XYZ Food Bank, I agree to the following principles of conduct in my personal, professional, and affiliated activities within and separate from this organization. I accept this responsibility willingly and for as long as I am associated with the XYZ Food Bank.

1. Abide by and work within the stated Articles of Incorporation and bylaws of this organization.
2. Exercise wisdom, good judgment, diligence, and stewardship in all my behavior as a representative of this organization.
3. Respect the principles of faith guiding the organization.
4. Protect the integrity and image of the organization.
5. Remain accountable to others who serve alongside me at the XYZ Food Bank.
6. Always give coworkers the benefit of the doubt in episodes of conflict.
7. Avoid using the organization for personal gain.
8. Refuse to discriminate in the delivery of my service at the XYZ Food Bank.
9. Consider all organizational resources as belonging first to God.
10. Treat all sensitive information shared as confidential within and outside the organization.

realistic is it that you will be able to attract the CEO of a major company and former chair of the Union Gospel Mission to your start-up board? Not very. But you believe in miracles, don't you? So after hours of prayer and careful listening, let your creative juices flow. Call your core leadership group together and brainstorm using these questions:

"Whom do you know that might be interested in our vision?"

"Whom should we ask to meet with to share our vision?"

"What high-profile leader can we name that has a spouse or children following in his or her philanthropic footsteps?'

"Who has employees that are encouraged to serve in this capacity?"

"Who is on maternity leave and may be interested in our vision?"

"What missionary is on furlough with some time to give?"

"What complementary national or international ministry might have donors in our area?"

"What large nonprofit organization has management staff who know our field?"

You get the idea—think creatively.

Step 5: Schedule Appointments to Share Your Vision

Don't invite anyone to serve on your board via telephone or e-mail. That is insulting to you and the person you are approaching. Show you take this seriously, more like a commission from God—which it is, after all. Instead, phone or e-mail for an appointment to get the person's advice on your new endeavor. Remember, people are flattered to be regarded as wise and experienced. Make yourself available on their timetable. Insist on buying their coffee, no matter how wealthy they might be. You are asking them for their valuable time; the least you can do is show your appreciation in this small way. Even if they turn you down for a position on your board, they can refer you to others whom you may not know. Your list will grow and expand just by sharing your vision with high-profile figures.

It may take months for you to actually get a meeting with the folks at the top of your list. That's OK—keep working your list. You'll become better at "the ask" the more you do it. Always refer to your board profile grid to ensure balance on your board. Don't stop pursuing high-profile leaders just because you think you have enough board members. Even after you are satisfied with your board makeup, you should still seek wisdom and guidance from experienced people. Remain teachable and curious about how you can do your work better. Your commitment to excellence will attract valuable advice and impress key individuals who will help you in other ways.

WHY YOU WANT EXPERIENCED BOARD MEMBERS

It's the invention of the wheel thing again. If you are not an expert in the operation of a nonprofit or don't have related education and experience, you need to have a couple of people who know how to lead a meeting according to *Robert's Rules* and all that. You need to have someone who can redirect conversation toward a productive end so that your time together is not wasted. Wasted time in board meetings is a sure way to lose your coworkers fast! You also want someone who has served on other boards and can bring stories of what worked and what didn't work in other situations. You need a few people who can read financial statements and understand their implications each month. Experienced board members are also more likely to accept the responsibility of fundraising because they have seen how it works in the past. They set the tone and pace for planning sessions and have realistic expectations of what could or should be accomplished in a given setting.

The justification for seeking out experienced board members is commonsense: there is no substitute for experience in any business pursuit, especially in the roles of nonprofit leadership. Typically, the driver of the organization is the founder, the visionary, the conceptual person. But as has already been pointed out, the vision and mission can be accomplished only with the proper leadership. That is the role of the board. Staff implement; the board leads, guides, and preserves the public trust.

Does this mean that there is no place for a novice on your board of directors? Not at all! Keep your profile grid in mind. Novice board members often have the energy and the availability to do the time-consuming stuff, like helping with grant applications, researching funding opportunities, attending functions where your presence is essential, reporting to other agencies about what your group is doing, and the like. A novice position would be a good place for an attorney or an accountant. This doesn't mean you should ask someone straight out of law school to handle your legal affairs. It just means that a younger professional is often eager to make a name in the community, and serving on a young board is a great way to help that process along! So, for example, a third-year CPA who is hoping to make an impression on the partners may be looking for a way to creatively build her account portfolio. You simply present the win-win situation. Just be sure to give her a clear job description delineating the tax schedule so that everyone knows what to expect from everyone else. Don't go overboard here and forget the importance of balance.

ADVISORY BOARDS

I love advisory boards. They're a great way to keep those high-profile folks involved in your work. If they don't have time to serve on your board of directors, ask them to serve on your advisory board. The membership of an advisory board is an additional list of names you can publish that lends credibility to your organization without demanding a lot of time or actual hands-on activity from board members. The advisory board can be as formal or informal as your situation allows. Its existence simply implies that these folks are willing to support your work in a lesser capacity than serving on the board of directors. They are a resource that you can go to for specific events or problems or for introductions to other potential helpers or investors. It's not unlikely that a person serving on your advisory board will be willing to move over to the board of directors after some time after having been impressed with the operations of a well-run organization that is accomplishing its mission.

Let me state it one last time: your organization is only as effective as its board of directors. That is why it's critical that you put lots of consideration, prayer, and attention into assembling the board. Each person on it should have a role to play. Rely on your experienced members to take the lead when unforeseen circumstances arise. No one should be there just taking up space on the roster.

LEGAL ISSUES: INCORPORATION, ACCOUNTING, INSURANCE

Once you have enough of a board in place—a minimum of three people who serve as officers, preferably six or seven—you can begin to delegate the tasks necessary to become fully incorporated, if you haven't already done so. I think it can be beneficial to wait until you have a board in place. These are matters that the board should address. They will become more fully invested in the organization if they have participated in the incorporation and legal process. If you have followed my recommendations on the balance of the board profile, you now have a lawyer in your midst and an accountant available for the financial details. It isn't important that your lawyer and accountant aren't experts in nonprofit structures; they just need to find someone who is. Often a large legal or accounting firm has at least one associate that does nonprofit work. Ask for an in-kind donation of his or her services. Your board will probably have to come up with the filing fees, which can run anywhere from $25 to $500, depending on your state. But this is a small portion of the true cost of preparing the incorporation.

Articles, Bylaws, and Annual Reports

There are do-it-yourself tool kits for each of these documents found on various Web sites through our links at www.josseybass.com/go/esau. But unless your board or advisory board includes a nonprofit lawyer and accountant, I recommend that you not go that route. It would be better to raise the funds to pay for the service or ask for an in-kind donation than to run the risk of misfiling or forgetting a deadline in your start-up phase. The cost for all this stuff varies from firm to firm. Shop around and get the word out that you are looking for help in this area. Often there is a member of your congregation who would be willing to do the work pro bono. You never know where help will come from. Most nonprofit lawyers have sample articles of incorporation and bylaws to get you started. You tweak the prototype to fit your organizational goals. (See Resources A and B.)

For example, the articles for all nonprofits state similar things. You could even refer to your church's articles of incorporation, which should be available to all members, from the church administrative staff. You can insert language that is specific to your program. The case with bylaws is similar but less universal; you need to be more specific in your bylaws. For example, if you intend to function as a community development corporation (CDC), you must state that in your bylaws. If you intend to work in partnership with the public school system, you need to include that as well. The bylaws also specify the term limits of your board members. As noted earlier, this is important—you need to decide on term limits to encourage participants' commitment and to prevent apathy and stagnation on your board. Turnover on a managed scale is healthy.

The articles and bylaws are filed with the state, which in turn submits them to the Internal Revenue Service. Then you need to file for a tax exemption, which is the part that takes time—up to six months in some states. Your donors will not be allowed to deduct their contributions until you have obtained your tax exemption. So, nonprofit incorporation is in fact a two-step process: filing articles and bylaws gets you an employer identification number (EIN), which is required on all grant applications and requests for funding, but you also need to obtain tax-exempt status, which allows others to give money to your organization and deduct it as a charitable contribution on their tax returns.

This process is greatly streamlined by working with licensed professionals, as already mentioned. They know just what forms to use and where to send them. They have contact numbers to follow up on the status of your filing, and they know what questions to ask and to whom those questions should be directed.

Quarterly and Annual Reports and Payroll Taxes

Although nonprofits are exempt from income taxes, we still have to file quarterly and annual reports with the state. Quarterly reports are simple one- or two-page forms that ask for financial information as a means of tracking how nonprofits are managing their funds. Annual reports are more extensive, sort of like your personal income taxes. They ask how much money you brought in, where it came from, and how it was spent. These reports can be prepared by the executive director, but in larger organizations, they're best left to an accountant, which is the main reason you want an accountant on your board.

You are responsible for payroll taxes if you have a staff and payroll expenses. Most start-up organizations don't have paid staff, or at least salaried staff, for several months, if not years. However, if you or any other contract employee receives any payment for work you do for the organization, you are required to report that as earned income on your tax return. Contract work is not taxed by your organization; it's simply listed in the program budget as a onetime fee-for-service expense.

Chances are you won't have to worry about payroll taxes for some time; but when the time comes, you must take payroll taxes seriously. (The accountant on your board should be able to handle them without much trouble.) I once worked in an organization that had to cease operations for failure to pay two years of payroll taxes for thirty employees. A nonprofit is not allowed to take funds allocated to specific programs from grant money and redirect them to other operational expenses. Most nonprofit donations are "designated funds," which means that the donor or grantor gave those funds to the organization for very specific uses. So unless you have a substantial account in your budget listed as "general operating funds," the overwhelming amount of your money must be used for programs. As you can imagine, it's hard to raise funds from a private donor to pay for delinquent tax liens. Don't run that risk!

Insurance

A fairly new development in the nonprofit realm is the issue of insurance. Today, nonprofit boards are protecting themselves with liability insurance as a matter of course. For smaller or start-up organizations, this practice is not as necessary. But as you grow and extend across a more diverse service landscape, the chances for lawsuits increases. And in our day of activist judges and controversial social trends, it is wise to purchase some amount of board liability insurance to protect your volunteers. I am sorry to say that this reality is particularly true for faith-based social ministries.

We'll focus more on the topic of faith-based rights and limitations in Chapter Six when we analyze the Charitable Choice laws. But for now, be aware that as faith-based ministries are acquiring government contracts in increasing numbers, we will see opposition by way of lawsuits until more extensive precedents are set. If you are operating under the radar screen, you are less of a target than the larger, intermediary nonprofits that are landing multimillion-dollar contracts with the government. So because we can expect this type of opposition and because we want to continue to attract experienced and effective board members and volunteers to our programs without fear of personal liability, we help ourselves by purchasing some amount of board insurance. Again, your professionals can take care of this for you when you are ready.

VOLUNTEERS

Many professionals in our field, myself included, consider volunteers the lifeblood of any nonprofit. Most secular and virtually all faith-based organizations could not afford to pay for the work accomplished by their volunteer force. Just think of some examples of the ministries with which you are familiar—a local food bank, a homeless shelter, a job training program held in your church . . . the list goes on forever! How could any of those programs survive and grow without committed, reliable volunteers manning the stations each day?

In fact, their significance is so profound that dozens of books have been published in the past decade on the issue of volunteer management. Volunteerism is an activity peculiar to Americans. Alexis de Tocqueville wrote about the American phenomenon of volunteerism and community associations in his 1835 observations of American life, *Democracy in America.* Our unique quality of commitment to social and civil society stems from the role of faith in the everyday life of most Americans and continues to impress the world even today.

The value of volunteers is no longer questioned. In fact, volunteers are a huge factor in government, corporate, and foundation grant awards. We are now expected to total up the thousands of hours of help that trained volunteers add to our programs and in some cases count those hours as matching funds. Today, many grant applications allow an organization to itemize the value of their volunteer base as donated hourly staff time, donated technical assistance, and professional in-kind consultation. Volunteers are a nonprofits' not-so-secret weapon when competing for state and local government social service contracts. Decision makers in key government positions are finally realizing that the best care for the hardest-to-serve populations is provided at the neighborhood level. The best behavioral tracking, accountability, and mentoring occur one-on-one in neighborhood after-school programs and church twelve-step program relationships. It is simply impossible to outgive God!

But with tremendous blessing comes responsibility. The better volunteer forces are well trained and well managed. Today, there are graduate courses offered in volunteer management because common sense teaches us that groups of people need guidance to work together, even if they do it for pleasure. Let's look briefly at some important and complex factors in managing volunteers.

Managing Volunteers

It doesn't matter if you're World Vision or a brand-new start-up: the way you handle your volunteers should be the same. Give them recognition, appreciation, and respect, and they'll keep coming back. Ignore them and take them for granted, and you'll forever be replacing them with a new crop, which is expensive and time-consuming. The most important principle to drill into your mind when dealing with volunteers is to *protect the relationship.* This is especially true in faith-based organizations. And it is even more important in the start-up phase, when you rely heavily on donated time because there is no budget for paid staff. Did you catch the term *donated time*? Think of your volunteers as donating their time, and you will appreciate them more—for what is our most precious commodity in today's culture but time? Everyone is too busy today, so when people offer to donate their time to your cause, they are truly offering you a gift. Don't take that lightly!

If you are trying to get a new social ministry off the ground, where are you most likely to go for volunteer help? Won't you go to your church friends? You have probably been talking about your latest project in small groups or with study buddies, so it's natural to let them know when you need some help. Be very careful. Protect your relationships by conducting yourself with integrity, and you'll have a wonderful time working with your friends. But treat them poorly or with a lack of love, honor, and respect, and the news will travel like wildfire throughout the church.

Nothing is worth damaging your relationships. No amount of good works can make up for destroyed friendships. How do I know? Personal experience has taught me a lot. I have seen churches and ministries devastated by relationship rifts. Can anyone honestly say this honors God and is worthy of His name? Is it God's design for churches and ministries to split over hurt feelings and for one faction to take up residence down the block? How can we expect our work to be fruitful and blessed when our leaders can't get along with our neighbors or coworkers?

Here are a few tips to protect your relationships with your volunteers, who are your co-laborers:

1. Follow the guidelines of job descriptions and contracts so that there are no surprise expectations on anyone's part.
2. Train volunteers thoroughly so that their work is productive.
3. Communicate clearly in matters of time, outcomes, and appreciation.
4. Give volunteers a certain amount of room to be creative in their work—that makes it more fun for them.

There are many great ideas for honoring your volunteers, including special lunches, printed certificates or awards handed out at a public function, and mentioning names in a newsletter with details of their service. (Additional ideas can be garnered from the links to volunteer Web sites at www.josseybass.com/go/esau.) The tough part for start-ups is finding the time and personnel to do this important task. But do it you must.

The most impressive volunteer recognition effort I have seen was at Willow Creek Community Church in Barrington, Illinois. This megachurch has at last count around twenty-five thousand members! Each member is expected to have a volunteer job in the church. The obvious question is, how does the staff go about recognizing all twenty-five thousand volunteers each year? The answer is *deliberately planned time management.* During the first week I attended a leadership conference at Willow Creek, I observed three different departments in the church—administration, food services, and child care. In each of these departments, each staff member was required to send out handwritten thank-you notes to each volunteer who served in his or her area of ministry before the week was out. That means that by Sunday, all thank-you notes for the previous six days had to be in the mail. Food service alone had an average of two hundred volunteers in any given week. So the small staff of about ten each had to get twenty notes written every week. I can tell you that each staff person I met had a stack of written and blank notes in his or her possession at all times during the week. What kind of impact do you think that has on Willow Creek's volunteer force? What kind of impact do you think the practice of thanking those volunteers has on the staff? That experience left a powerful impression on me. And I know that the exercise helps remind the staff to be thankful for the precious people who come to serve each week. Does that practice work? I'd say so: most of the volunteers in food service had been working in that capacity for several years.

Whatever you decide to do to recognize your volunteers, the important thing to remember is to be genuine. Even the smallest gesture of thanks is plenty if the recipient knows it is sincere. *Never* take volunteers for granted! If you do, word gets around pretty fast, and soon you are left with no one to cover your bases.

Training Volunteers

Training volunteers can be as important as training paid staff. Job descriptions should be written and contracts signed by each volunteer, whether they are board members, computer trainers, or child care workers (see the example in Exhibit 3.4). A signed contract and a written job description let volunteers know that you take them seriously and will treat them with dignity. A weekly or monthly schedule also helps everyone plan responsibly. It shows that you consider your volunteers on a par with staff while they are serving and worthy of your attention and praise.

But how do you go about teaching people a job they're doing for only an hour a week? Is the effort really worth the investment of your time? The answer is always yes, for several reasons. First, the role of a volunteer is to accomplish some task that you and staff need to have done, but finding the time to do it is challenging. So training the volunteer frees up your time to do other things. Second, thoroughly preparing a helper to perform an important task adds value to that person's life; the person is choosing to help out because he or she enjoys it. So the

Exhibit 3.4
Sample Volunteer Job Description

Mission of Hope

Volunteer Job Description

Position:	Educational volunteer serving as after-school tutor for homeless children
Duties:	Volunteer is committing to tutor at-risk children from 5 to 12 years of age. Time commitment is 3 hours per session, one day per week, to be mutually agreed with the Mission of Hope staff. Tutor sessions will be conducted at the Mission facility at 555 West Main Street. Tutors are expected to attend one 6-hour training seminar offered on certain Saturdays throughout the year. A final test will be administered to determine the tutor's skill level in anticipation of matching the tutor with students. Tutors are expected to spend half their time with the student working on reading skills and half the time working on math skills. A 15-minute break with a small meal will be shared between subjects. Informal testing will be conducted by the tutor periodically during the tutoring relationship to determine the increased knowledge of the student. Additional time may be added to the tutor's schedule upon mutual agreement of the Mission of Hope and the volunteer tutor.
Materials:	All tutoring program materials will be provided by the Mission of Hope. Volunteers are not required to bring any extra materials from their personal stock.
Absenteeism:	In the event of illness or other inability to attend a tutoring session, the volunteer is required to notify the Mission of Hope staff in a timely manner and to make every effort to find a replacement for the missed session.
Dates:	The volunteer's time commitment will begin on October 1 and continue until the last week of the school year, around June 12.

____________________ ____________________

Volunteer signature Mission of Hope director

situation is, as it must be, win-win. When volunteers begin to question the value of the work they are being handed or feel that it is merely busywork, their attitude and reliability will begin to decline. Third, training your volunteer ensures that you will not have to redo the work after the volunteer leaves. If you find this happening, the instructions for the job were inadequate. Fourth, happy, well-trained volunteers will almost always bring along friends! They will be talking about the organization everywhere they go, and soon others will be curious enough to join in.

Volunteers who have proved to be dedicated and reliable may be ready to assume more authority over more demanding work. They may become good trainers of new volunteers, which takes that job off the shoulders of staff. After some time at the job, veteran volunteers may have some good ideas to improve the way the work could be done. Eventually, in established organizations, it is not uncommon for regular volunteers to join the staff on a part-time or full-time basis.

Volunteer Training Programs

Your volunteer training doesn't have to be a sophisticated weeklong process if you are just starting up. Obviously, you are operating in "feel as you go" mode most of the time. But even starting out, there are some important points your helpers should be trained on.

1. Make all volunteers aware of the big picture of what you are ultimately trying to accomplish. Ask them to memorize your mission statement. They need to know who the board members are, who major contributors are, what other programs are you partnering with, the amount of your operating budget, how many folks your program is serving and where, and background details of how the program began. Give them a fact sheet with this information so that they can share it with anyone who asks.

2. Interview volunteers and ask what their interests are. What attracted them to your program? What kinds of work have they done in the past? What special skills do they have that you could use in your program—computer programming, public relations, teaching or training, writing, and so on? Try to match your volunteers' skills with the jobs you give them. Ask if they see a place in the organization where their skills could best be utilized. State what your needs are and see if there's a good match. This creates the win-win situation.

3. Describe the job or task you have in mind for the volunteers you interview. Don't assume that they will be thrilled with the work. Show them how the work needs to be done and why. They need to know the significance of the work. Help them succeed by providing a script that could read something like this:

> We need these phone calls made today because we're having our fundraiser dinner next week. If our guests don't have it on their calendar, this will be a good reminder. If they do, we need to know if they prefer chicken or salmon for their meal. We also want to know if they have invited any other guests so that we have name tags ready at the door. Thank them for their participation or their time. If they're not planning to attend, ask them if they would consider making a contribution anyway over the phone. Before you hang up, ask them if they have any questions about the program. Then, before you say goodbye, ask if there is anything you could be praying for for them this week. That leaves the potential supporter feeling cared for and positive about our program and hence more likely to participate in the future.

This is a simple training process that should take about four minutes. Be sure to ask volunteers if they have any questions. Ask if they are comfortable saying all the things you want them to say. If they are not sure they can say everything the way you described it, ask how they would prefer to say it. Then agree on what they'll say so that each of you understands exactly what will be said and are satisfied with the conversation. Show them precisely how to record their findings and results. Thank the volunteers sincerely and let them know that you think they'll do a great job!

4. Encourage your volunteers to ask questions. Impress on them that it's better to ask and get a clear answer than to speculate and assume something that's incorrect. This is especially true in the public realm. If your volunteers represent your organization in public, at community meetings, at church functions, or at any venue where people are introduced to your work, the volunteers need to feel OK with sometimes saying, "I don't know, but I'll find that answer for you." Many problems occur when a well-meaning volunteer speaks out of turn and says something incorrect. The damage goes far beyond the inaccurate information: it cuts to the very credibility of your work. The guess at an answer could indicate to another that your organization hasn't thought through some critical details, such as how to present yourself in public. It also discourages volunteers when you have to correct them later. This principle goes back to the most important thing: protect your relationships, including your future ones.

5. Train yourself, your staff, and your volunteers to seek restoration. When a situation occurs that causes hurt feelings or a serious rift, do whatever it takes immediately to restore that relationship. If a problem arises between a volunteer and a staff member or between two volunteers, drop everything and fix it! Don't let it sort itself out—it never does. The relationship will be damaged and will color subsequent interactions until one or both parties disassociate from the organization. It's better to stop all work on a project if there is a relational problem. It's far better to be late on a printing deadline, for example, if there is disagreement between coworkers than to go forward and allow disharmony to persist.

Note that these training suggestions do not necessarily apply to all nonprofit organizations. I believe that faith-based organizations are called to some different standards. One of those differences is the way we conduct our relationships and volunteer practices. If these suggestions seem eccentric or very different from your previous experience, that's fine. They are only suggestions. But however you design your volunteer activities, please don't forget the most important issue: protecting your relationships.

BUDGETING 101

If you dread the entire realm of finance and budgets, you are not alone. Thousands of other professional people break into a cold sweat when they have to discuss or read budgets in a meeting. The best way to deal with finances and budgets, as I mentioned earlier, is to find a talented person to handle that responsibility for you. Even so, if you are the team leader, executive director, or chief visionary of your project or organization, it is necessary that you learn to read a budget.

This task doesn't have to be painful; you can pick up a lot just by asking questions in a meeting or asking a CPA to walk you through a profit-and-loss statement, a balance sheet, or an organizational budget over lunch.

There are many different kinds of budgets that every business uses. Those for nonprofits are the same, if not more complicated. Standard project budgets are essential for each project or program you want to initiate (for examples, see Exhibits 3.5 and 3.6). An annual budget that is approved by your board of directors is also pretty basic. Where things get murky is when you start applying for grants or foundation, government, or corporate support. When submitting a foundation or corporate proposal, your budget needs to include things like the value of your in-kind contributions, matching funds, and volunteer staff time. It is a real blessing to be able to include these line items because they increase the amount your organization brings

Exhibit 3.5
Sample Preliminary Budget

Sunshine Summer Camp

Preliminary Budget

Summary

The Sunshine Summer Camp exists to provide unique outdoor activities for children aged 10 to 15 in a rustic setting with a diverse peer group. Our aim is for children to leave our camp with improved communication skills; a deeper understanding of themselves, others, and the world around them; and fond memories of outdoor fun. Sunshine operates on a "bare-bones budget" intentionally to teach children that fun does not need to cost a lot of money.

Camping opportunities are one- or two-week stays during the months of July and August. The following breakdown illustrates how camp times can be purchased (price per camper):

Week 1	Week 2	Week 3	Week 4	Week 5	Week 6
$100	$100	$100	$100	$100	$100

Each week can accommodate 100 campers comfortably, each paying $100 per week.

Total income from tuition = $60,000

Total expenses for six weeks = $100,000

This schedule brings our budget to break-even status.

However, we can accommodate up to 120 campers per week with somewhat crowded yet safe conditions. Should this occur, Sunshine Summer Camp would realize a small surplus.

Exhibit 3.6
Sample Projected Budget

FB Capacity Center

Projected Budget

Income	**Year 1**	**Year 2**	**Year 3**
Contributions			
Foundations	75,000	75,000	100,000
Corporate	30,000	30,000	30,000
Individuals	10,000	20,000	30,000
Churches	20,000	20,000	20,000
Earned Income			
Federal contracts (@ 10,000 each)	30,000	60,000	100,000
State contracts (@ 10,000 each)	50,000	100,000	200,000
Membership training	5,000	20,000	40,000
Totals	$220,000	$275,000	$520,000

Expenses	**Year 1**	**Year 2**	**Year 3**
Salaries			
Executive director	60,000	60,000	61,800
Technical and communications director (0.75 FTE)	50,000	50,000	51,500
Administrative support	28,000	28,000	28,840
Events coordinator	0	0	30,000
Benefits (@ 22%)	30,360	30,360	37,870
Total salaries	168,360	168,360	210,010
Travel (× 2)	4,000	6,000	7,000
Parking (× 3)	3,600	3,600	4,800
Mileage (× 2)	2,500	2,500	2,500
Office			
Equipment	10,000	0	3,000
Supplies and printing	7,000	7,000	7,000
Contractual			
Rent	24,000	25,000	26,000
Accounting and legal services	10,000	8,000	6,000
Phone and DSL	2,500	2,500	2,500
Training sessions (48)	4,800	4,800	4,800
Totals	$236,760	$227,760	$273,610

to the total budget. They offset the bottom line in a way that makes the project seem less risky for the donor. Including in-kind and volunteer dollar values is subjective and left to you, the applicant. But be prepared to back up your calculations if you are asked to do so.

Government grant budgets are different. Many times the request for proposal (RFP) guidelines will designate an amount you may attribute to in-kind and volunteer value. They also dictate how much you may include in your budget for "indirect" costs, such as employee benefits. You will find at least one page of a "budget narrative." This is your opportunity to defend your line items and expenses by explaining, for example, exactly why your personnel amount reaches the maximum allowed. You are also expected to defend why and how your budget increases or decreases over time—due to a onetime equipment purchase or initial travel expenses, for example (see Exhibit 3.7).

Exhibit 3.7
Sample Federal Grant Budget Narrative

Your notes must demonstrate that the expense is *adequate, reasonable,* and *necessary.*

ABC Faith Center

Personnel

For each position, provide narrative for each point below.

Position 1: Technical

- Executive director, responsible for managing capacity center, liaison for FBOs, CBOs, government, business, funding base, other resources. Will represent constituency in community, provide leadership and guidance to grassroots organizations in their efforts to expand operations, and collaborate with complementary services. Will also generate opportunities and act as conduit for government and private contracts by raising the visibility of FBOs across sectors and encouraging implementation of best practices.
- Full-time salary request: $60,000 annually
- This position is key in establishing a capacity center in Seattle, raising awareness of FBOs, and maintaining good relations across the sectors.

Position 2: Technical

- Chief strategic consultant, responsible for technical functions and communications within the capacity center and among constituency; troubleshooter for FBOs and CBOs in region; identifies and proposes strategies for specific needs within organizations to build capacity and increase effectiveness. Conducts on-site evaluations weekly as needed.
- Three-quarters-time salary request: $50,000 annually
- This position translates the goals of the capacity center into tangible outcomes while improving relations and integrating services of FBOs.

Position 3: Technical

- Administrative support staff, responsible for administrative details in capacity center; handles initial inquiries, phones, word and data processing, establishes filing system, database, general office maintenance.
- Half-time salary request: $28,000 annually
- This position is necessary to support projects and maintain operations of the capacity center and to ensure that all work initiated by staff is professionally completed in a timely manner.

Fringe Benefits

- Full-time @ 22%, 12% for medical insurance, 10% payroll taxes
- Part-time @ 14%, 4% choice of insurance or other, 10% payroll taxes

Travel

- DHHS conference: 4 days @ $150/day for 1 person includes food and lodging, airfare = $150 round trip
- CCDA Conference in Los Angeles: $150 food and lodging for 2 people, airfare = $600 round trip for 2 people
- D.C. training: $150 food and lodging for 2 people, airfare = $1,000 round trip for 2 people
- Mileage: 34 cents/mile @ 200 miles/week = $68/week = $272/month = $3,264/year

Exhibit 3.7
Sample Federal Grant Budget Narrative, Cont'd.

Equipment

- 3 computers with printers @ $1,500 each = $4,500
- 3 phones compatible with existing system @ $200 each = $600
- Copier/fax on monthly lease = $600/year (est.)

Equipment 1

- Name of equipment, maker, model number, etc. (or similar)
- Use of equipment in relation to capacity center's purpose
- How cost was calculated and the competitive bidding process that you used (or will use) to identify the equipment

Equipment 2

- Name of equipment, maker, model number, etc. (or similar)
- Use of equipment in relation to capacity center's purpose
- How cost was calculated and the competitive bidding process that you used (or will use) to identify the equipment

Supplies

Identify all items that will be purchased under $5,000; group items such as paper goods together in general categories.

Category 1

- Initial letterhead design and printing = $500; 6 reams/year @ $15 = $90 + tax
- Business cards, initial newsletter, etc.

Category 2

- Small office supplies, copy paper = 8 reams/year @ $20 = $160
- Calendars, markers, white boards, binders, files, Post-it Notes, staplers, etc.

Identify in the following section whether the item is for technical assistance or subgranting.

Contractual

List all contracts for services and subgranting here.

- Accountant and legal fees for 501(c)(3) incorporation (Admin.)
- NP financial accounting training sessions: 4/month @ $100 (Tech.)
- Subgranting (no dollar amount budgeted) would be awarded for best practices such as creating Web site, e-newsletters, collaborative efforts, attending training, offering sites for training, requesting evaluations

Other

- Rent: $3,000/month = $36,000/year
- Phone and DSL = $1,600/year
- Postage = $60/month = $720/year

Indirect Charges

- Depreciation on equipment: $100/month = $1,200/year

Program Income

Nonfederal Resources

- Describe the sources for your matching funds for each amount, and be prepared to include letters of commitment to support these commitments and plans. Matching without backup letters is unlikely.

Once you get the hang of preparing nonprofit budgets, the anxiety diminishes. But I still believe it is best to ask an accountant or bookkeeper for help with budgets. There is simply too much at stake to submit a sloppy budget for public or donor review. Of course, your board should be approving budgets each month at a board meeting. This keeps everyone up-to-date on the financial health of the organization, no matter how much or how little money you have. You can find more examples by going to some of the many Web sites for nonprofit professionals listed on our Web site at www.josseybass.com/go/esau.

Sometimes you may find it useful to insert a basic budget in a draft service contract to address the matter of funding without presenting a full-fledged project budget (see Exhibit 3.8). Because the terms of the contract will probably change before becoming final, such a tentative budget gives the parties a general understanding of the estimated cost of a project during the negotiation phase without committing anyone to a binding financial arrangement.

Once you have a solid team in place and all participants know what is expected of them and what they can expect from their participation in the larger scheme of things, you are ready to begin the process of serious planning and fundraising. As you initiate the planning process, it is good to encourage your team (board, volunteers, potential staff) by reminding them that their input and expertise are of the utmost importance and utility in the planning and fundraising stages of your organization's evolution. Key decisions in these areas will chart the course of your work for the next several years. We begin to examine that process in Chapter Four.

Exhibit 3.8
Sample Contract for Service

Purpose

This document outlines terms of agreement between Contractor (contractor) and Malachi, chairman of the Old Testament Foundation (consignor), for a period of six months. All work will be performed by Contractor, under the name of Contract A, a nonprofit organization in formative stage. Any employee benefits during the six-month contract period mutually agreed by Malachi and the Old Testament Foundation board of directors shall be the responsibility of Contractor.

Expected Deliverables

1. Initiate the incorporation process; work with attorneys, accountants, the IRS, and board members to complete this process as soon as possible.
2. Build a network of relationships within the faith-based community to raise awareness of the Old Testament alliance as a regional hub for the dissemination of valuable information.
3. Support the governing board's partnership with administration as directed by the chair.
4. Maintain relations with and contribute to the success of the national Old Testament alliance; act as liaison on behalf of all project partners.
5. Facilitate and commission work groups designed to meet the needs of the regional faith-based social service leadership and direct-service staff.
6. Develop relationships and working contracts with government entities that will lead to partnerships and collaborative efforts within and beyond the faith-based community.
7. Manage staff under the contract as positions are added, to be determined by board consensus.
8. Manage financial matters under the contract, develop monthly budgets, track expenses, pursue and secure funding whenever possible, file quarterly reports, balance accounts, and purchase supplies as needed.
9. Investigate office location possibilities after three months; work with the manager to determine needs and conditions of an eventual lease.
10. Conduct government-sponsored conferences as scheduled; negotiate to increase the number of conference contracts.
11. Conduct regional training sessions on management best practices as recognized by the national Old Testament alliance.

The foregoing responsibilities are classified as "capacity-building" efforts that will increase the effectiveness and reach of the faith-based community, as prescribed in the mission of both the Old Testament Foundation and Contractor A. Realistically, this description requires the full-time employment of several people. However, in light of current budget constraints, the following schedule is proposed for the initial six months:

Exhibit 3.8
Sample Contract for Service, Cont'd.

Date	Nov. 2005	Dec. 2005	Jan. 2006	Feb. 2006	Mar. 2006	Apr. 2006
Hours	100	100	125	150	150	150
Amount	$2,500	$2,500	$3,125	$3,750	$3,750	$3,450

Rates and Terms

The above schedule assumes a beginning rate of $25 per hour and an ending rate in April of $23 per hour. No benefits are included in these terms, and Contractor A agrees to be responsible for all income taxes. At the end of six months, this contract will be renegotiated, based on progress and conditions at that time.

Contractor agrees to accept payment for this contract from Malachi and the Old Testament Foundation by December 1, 2006.

Hold Harmless Clause

All parties involved agree to hold Contractor harmless from any action, claim, cost, liability, or damages arising out of or in connection with any work performed under this contractual agreement.

______________________________ ______________________________

Contractor Date Malachi Date
Old Testament Foundation

chapter
FOUR

Fundraising with a Plan

How Much Money Do You Need and How Will You Get It?

Perhaps you have already begun the process of looking for funds to pay the costs related to your service. The planning practices set forth in this chapter will help you determine how much money it will take to do what you want to do and how to leverage those dollars for greater benefit. Planning is the secret; but we'll also discuss where and how to dig up some money!

As a person of faith, you are well acquainted with the concept of "counting the cost before you attempt a job." The phrase refers to the obstacles and unforeseen struggles that inevitably accompany the commitment to sacrificially serve others. Counting the cost is not only a principle of common sense but also a principle of good stewardship and obedience. These are the foundations on which you will build your organization or expand it for greater reach. Ignore these principles of common sense and good stewardship, and you will invite failure to any project you attempt, philanthropic or otherwise. But obey them and you could enjoy success beyond your wildest expectations.

Remember, the need is great (the harvest is ripe) but the workers are few. If you follow some basic steps in setting up your program, you will model good stewardship and avoid wasting time and resources. Counting the cost translates into careful planning. As people of faith, we are held to a higher standard in our business conduct and interpersonal relationships. A wonderful way to demonstrate our commitment to stewardship is through planning and fundraising. This is not a place to cut corners. Once your planning has taken some form and shape, you can begin the fundraising process.

Be forewarned that if you try to raise funds before your house is in order, your potential donors and investors will perceive only a "well-intentioned servant" running around enthusiastically with some plans that may or may not materialize. Imagine that picture; it will help you understand how seriously you must take this whole business of planning and fundraising.

So let's assume you agree to follow the basic formula of counting the cost in order to answer your call. Where should you start? Creating a plan is your first step toward realizing your goal. There are many ways to create plans and many types of plans you will need as you chart your course. I'll list the most important ones here and give several examples you can use individually or in a team meeting. Each example is unique. That's because each organization and each project is unique. Do what seems right for you.

Keep in mind that the topics of planning and fundraising are significant enough to address in separate university graduate-level courses. Consider this discussion an introduction to the issues and not a comprehensive presentation of the pillars of nonprofit management.

Working through these tools will get you off to a great start. When you reach a point where you need more sophisticated material, you may consider attending one of the many community workshops offered by the United Way or other training sponsors in your area. There are also experts and consultants you can hire to help you plan once you have your operations humming along nicely. As you should expect, however, hiring outside experts can be expensive. Check your local community college for nonprofit instructors, and use Resource E at the back of the book and our Web site (www.josseybass.com/go/esau) to track down some professional contacts.

Winston Churchill once said, "We make a living by what we get, but we make a life by what we give." As you prepare for planning and fundraising, always remember to *keep the big picture in mind.* There are countless examples throughout history of servant-leaders who answered their call and so pleased the One Who Called that the floodgates opened and their storehouses could not contain all that was bestowed upon them.

The *New York Times* reported on June 22, 2004, that Americans gave a staggering $240.7 billion to charitable organizations in 2003. This is quite surprising in light of the sluggish economy and the fear of international terrorism. Citing figures from

Giving USA, a publication of the American Association of Fundraising Counsel, Stephanie Strom reported that this equaled 2.2 percent of the nation's gross domestic product for that year and that 86.4 percent was given to religious organizations.

Americans are generous not only with their hard-earned dollars but also with their time. According to INDEPENDENT SECTOR's *Comprehensive Report on Giving and Volunteering in the United States,* released in October 2002, some 83.9 million Americans—44 percent of the adult population—volunteer an average of twenty-two hours each month. Three out of four of those volunteers belong to religious organizations, and one-fourth of all volunteer hours go to religious organizations. Ours is a better country because people step in, roll up their sleeves, and do what needs to be done to solve problems at the community level.

As you begin the process of planning the structure and course of your faith-based nonprofit, be encouraged by these numbers. Clearly, financial partners are out there, eager to support your work. Your job is to give them something they can understand, promote, and support with their time and money. Do your job well, and they will respond!

THE MANY STAGES OF PLANNING

In a sense, you have already been planning if you have established your board of directors and volunteer force. You have figured out some of your needs for leadership. You may have written your mission, vision, and values statements, which are also a type of planning. Program planning and strategic planning simply take that process to the next levels. Recall from Chapter Two the image of the house with a foundation (representing values), structure (mission), and appealing exterior (vision). Now is your chance to fill in the gaps with specifics.

Years ago, the typical method of corporate planning was called long-range planning. This method fell short for nonprofits because it focused on goals as distant as ten years down the road and didn't provide enough detail regarding such questions as "Why are we doing this?" and "How do we get there?" Today, the most effective planning model is the *strategic plan,* which extends out about three years and is built around mission, vision, and values. The strategic planning method allows us to plan according to our philosophy and adjust for unforeseen developments that inevitably occur. This fine-tuning may sound intimidating, but once you jump into the process, it is really fun. This process allows you to stand on the watchtower with your mission, vision, and values statements in hand and see where you want to go with them.

Nonprofit guru John Bryson defined strategic planning as a "disciplined effort to produce fundamental decisions and actions that shape and guide what an organization . . . is, what it does, and why it does it" (*Strategic Planning for Public and Nonprofit Organizations,* 1995).

In Chapter One, you completed a SWOT analysis, working through your strengths, weaknesses, opportunities, and threats. You identified your stakeholders and established some realities from which you can now move forward. Your strategic plan will give you guideposts and confidence to push through your designated objectives while remaining faithful to your mission and vision. Of course, as with every other detail of your ministry, the planning process must be preceded by lots of prayer, maybe some fasting, and a substantial amount of listening for spiritual direction.

In an established company, church, or larger nonprofit, strategic planning can take on a formal and even scientific dimension. Outside consultants are brought in to mediate the process, which can begin with a staff retreat and not end for the next eight to twelve months. Often such exercises are conducted in anticipation of a capital campaign, a lengthy project to raise funds for a new building or capital improvements to existing facilities. Sometimes major donors want to see a strategic plan before committing any support.

For younger or start-up organizations, the process may be more fluid and free-form. Many resources for strategic planning research and study are listed on our Web site, www.josseybass.com/go/esau. Here are some helpful tips:

- Expect confusion at first.
- Allow time for all team members to be heard.
- Stay on task; minimize the rabbit trails.
- Don't be afraid of what you don't understand.
- Revise when needed.
- Be accepting of a lengthy process.
- Work toward your preferred outcomes.
- End up with a road map, not a bible.

WHO SHOULD BE ON THE PLANNING TEAM?

Your entire leadership team or board of directors should participate in the planning process. If that group is large, say, more than ten people, you may want to assign four to six people from the team to serve on a planning committee. Then, if you have not already done so, make a list of stakeholders for your program. Include anyone who influences or is affected by the work you do or want to do.

For example, a list of possible stakeholders for an after-school tutoring program might look like this:

Your students	Your volunteers
Your students' parents	Your facility management or host
Your students' siblings	Your leadership team
Your students' schoolteachers	The PTA
The school principal	The school board
The next school students will attend	Neighborhood church representatives

Next, select two or three participants from this list to invite onto the planning committee. Explain that the process may take up to six months, but they may come for an introductory meeting to decide if they can commit to that time frame.

Then ask one or two potential funders to join you. People with experience in this process will be a real asset. A final group of ten to twelve is ideal. That way you can divide the work into subcategories and cover more territory in a shorter amount of time. Once each subgroup has accomplished its task, the entire group can meet to discuss a few items in one meeting instead of using up all of a weekly meeting's time for only one item.

There are some basic steps to follow that vary with the size and history of the organization. Established organizations often have substantial past issues that they need to correct or address, and the strategic plan is their method of doing so. But a new organization starting from zero rarely has baggage or image problems to deal with. So pull out your SWOT list from Chapter One, and begin to think about how to set the stage in order to accomplish what you want to do. It is also helpful if you give your team a deadline—a time frame or preliminary schedule will help people stay focused and productive. For example, you may want to complete your first draft of a strategic plan by the end of your fiscal year.

STARTING THE BALL ROLLING

Once you have your team assembled and you have a preliminary schedule, it is time to get going! Be aware that your meetings will seems disorganized and perhaps unproductive until you hit your stride. It may take two or three meetings to feel like you're actually accomplishing something. That's OK. Part of the process is learning how to work together, crafting a detailed strategy for accomplishing your short-, medium-, and long-term goals. Nothing is chiseled in stone. Your group is unique and must find its sea legs like every other group that has attempted this process. If you persevere and don't give up, you will have a plan that you will be satisfied with and proud to share with others.

If you are not using a consultant, your meetings should be led by a trusted stakeholder. This person will use lots of poster paper and colored markers to record every thought or suggestion that is mentioned. Normally, the last step of each meeting will be to boil all comments down to three or four acceptable items, depending on which topic you are addressing at that time.

Exhibit 4.1 suggests a six-step outline for creating your strategic plan. Simply insert your organization's and participants' names and attach dates to your meeting times where appropriate.

1. Conduct a focus group to identify the most significant issues for your organization or program that affect your work and challenge your success in accomplishing your mission. It may take two or three meetings just to arrive at four or five issues that your team agrees to tackle. That focus group can present its findings to the larger group, thereby abbreviating the process a bit.

2. Hold a planning retreat to allow the board to develop broad strategies to address these issues and challenges over the next year or two. Broad strategies are general ideas that help connect solutions to the challenges. These strategies should be expressed generally but clearly so that in the event of staff or volunteer turnover, a new person could easily jump in.

3. Draft a preliminary plan that attaches specific actions and tasks to each of the broad strategies to address the issue and incorporate it into the organizational culture. Choose three or four actions for each strategy, and assign a staff or volunteer position to the task. Give each task a completion date, and assign a responsible staff or board supervisor for each. These actions should all be completed within the two-year time frame.

4. Hold a combined meeting or retreat to refine the plan. All projected staff, board members, and significant volunteers should attend this meeting. Create a chart or table listing all activities in the specific categories of service, such as job training, food delivery, youth mentoring, finance, administration, or fundraising, with a designated person responsible and a projected completion date for each. This chart should include as much detail as possible so as to help resolve ambiguities that might arise later. Accountability should be assigned by position and proper title, allowing for staff and volunteer turnover. This ensures that the plan won't fall apart if personnel changes occur.

5. Implement the plan. Assign the specific duties and prepare a calendar of expected completion dates. Write a comprehensive report recounting the process and justifying all strategies and actions to be performed over the life of the plan. Include anticipated challenges and the methods of addressing those challenges. This report becomes the strategic plan that you will use to build budgets (like the one in Exhibit 4.2), send to interested parties and prospective donors, and refer to regularly in staff and board meetings for direction, motivation, and evaluation.

6. Celebrate with and inform all important people of your plan. Commemorate the unveiling of your plan with an event—large or small—that acts as a demarcation between the past and the future of your organization. Invite all stakeholders and any new potential partners or investors you want to share your work with. Print out the strategic plan, which will probably run to several pages, including colored charts and some photographs, and pass it around. Thank all participants by name and mention their contribution, with humor if possible. Make it a big deal—because it is!

PROJECT PLANNING

A second necessary planning exercise for any group is the development of a project plan. This is a much simpler process than developing the strategic plan because you're really dealing with just one element within your organization. If you are in your start-up or information-gathering phase, you may want to work up a project plan first to see how well you and your team do with a basic planning assignment. When you think about this type of planning, it is no different from the way you teach a Sunday school class or run a support group. You decide what information has to be covered by when, and then you devise a plan to accomplish that work. It's nothing fancy or complicated. The difference is that when you are dealing with an organizational goal or project, you are working in a relationship of trust with your clients, constituents, or board of directors. Busy people who are investing in your work need help with accountability. You need to have your plans in writing so that they can be measured, evaluated, and accounted for. (Evaluation will be discussed in Chapter Eight.)

Exhibit 4.1
Sample Strategic Plan: A Six-Step Schedule of Events

Step	Time Required	Completion Date	Participants	Location and Budget	Reporter	Action to Be Taken	Other Information
1. Focus groups	Two days	Jan. 20, 2005	10–20 stakeholders	Board office	TBA	Organization analysis	Also conducted in Vietnam
2. Board planning retreat	1.5 days over a weekend	Feb. 20, 2005	Entire board of directors	Sunshine Beach Conference Center, $500.00	TBA	Internal evaluation—see outline	Best to use a consultant
3. Drafting a preliminary plan	Two weeks to prepare, two weeks to review	Mar. 20, 2005	Designated champion and founder, LaRelle C.	Home offices	Champion and LaRelle	Compile data, draft preliminary plan	Contact reporters with suggestions
4. Combined retreat and refinement of the plan	One full day	Apr. 20, 2005	Board of directors and focus group participants	Sunshine Beach Conference Center, $500.00	TBA	Revise, edit, and draft final document	Joint group may require extra time

5. Implementation	One month to delegate tasks	May 20, 2005	Board of directors	Regular meeting place	Champion and LaRelle	List all goals, tasks, point people, timelines, and budgets	Allow until June 20 to complete this step (= six months since launch)
6. Celebration and information	June 20, 2005 (six-month mark)	June 30, 2005	All stakeholders and potential partners	TBA, $3,000	TBA	Plan party, prepare executive summary	Use this as an opportunity to increase awareness of the organization
	End of process			Total spent: $4,000–$5,000		Continue to circulate executive summary	Schedule annual review of plan

Project planning consists mostly of applying common sense to the accomplishment of your goal. You may have more success with this type of planning if you work backward from your goal and plug in specific objectives, dates, and names of people responsible for the tasks. Decide the completion date you are striving for, and then put everything else in place to make completion possible by that date.

Make a list of who does what. Then discuss where the holes are and how they should be filled in. If you don't have the capacity to fill in all the blanks right away, you may need to pare down your goals or restructure the project to fit your resources. As always, be creative in your solutions, and stretch your team to "shoot for the moon" in pursuing your goal. If you start your planning and realize that you need to personalize or add another category to fit your work, go right ahead and do that. You are on the road to planning success!

CASE STATEMENT

Another step in planning is to prepare yourself for questions your potential donors will ask or may not ask but will want to have answers to. It is not necessary to have completed your strategic plan before you set out to solicit support from individuals. But you will want to write up a short case statement, which is a basic document stating what you do, whom you serve, and why people should give you money to do it. It's your chance to tell your story in an effective way that invites your friends and contacts to participate with you. It can be as complete or as sketchy as you want it to be. Some elaborate case statements for established nonprofits can run to twenty or more pages with color charts, photographs, and stories of changed lives.

Obviously, if you are just starting out, such an elaborate case statement is neither possible nor necessary. A two- to three-page description of your program, along with your mission, vision, and values statements, will suffice. Later, as you develop your ministry and depending on the budget you have drafted as a result of your project plan or other planning tools you have created, you can begin the process of *resource development,* or fundraising.

There are other types of methods you will encounter as you jump into the realm of planning. Some will work better for you than others. Just be comfortable knowing that different methods work better than others, depending on the dynamics of your work and your team. The beauty of faith-based social ministry is that each project and program has its unique niche and process. Rarely are two exactly alike.

Your planning process will reflect your individual style and approach. But developing your strategic plan, project plan, and case statement will get you off and running as you develop and expand your ministry.

I hope that engaging in these activities will enrich all who participate and provide your organization with a clear, concise, practical strategy to lead you into your preferred future. Once you have a project plan, a case statement, and perhaps the start of a strategic plan, you can figure out how much it will all cost. The rest of this chapter explains the various types of fundraising in which nonprofits may engage.

AN INTRODUCTION TO FUNDRAISING

I mentioned earlier that the topics in this chapter are ordinarily covered in extensive graduate-level courses taught by seasoned professionals. Fundraising is an enormous wheel with many different spokes. Keep in mind that finding the money to pay for your work is a full-time job. We can't explore all the specifics here, but we'll discuss the most common methods and point you to other resources through our Web site, www.josseybass.com/go/esau.

It is unrealistic to think that just because you run a great program that serves folks in need, people with money will flock to you with large donations in repeating and increasing amounts. *That never happens!* Nor does it happen that just because you have started a program at your church, your friends and major church contributors will automatically support your work. Friends may toss you an initial gift to get you started, but they will expect to see "significant outcomes" before they commit to supporting your work over the long term.

Another serious matter that needs to be addressed is the common problem that accompanies a lot of faith-based work: the issue of *expectations.* Some people in the faith community have gained a reputation for arrogantly expecting others to donate goods and services just because we are "faith-based." I have heard embarrassing stories of businesses or professionals not being paid for services they have rendered to ministry leaders or other "church people," who justify their failure to pay by saying, "They should understand that I am doing the Lord's work." Another common excuse some "do-gooders" use for not paying bills runs along the lines of "He's a Christian doctor, so he should give me his services for free." Today, many professionals avoid working with people of faith because they have found them to be less than ethical.

Protect your relationships, your own reputation, and the larger field of social ministry by not expecting others to forgive your business debts. Operate with integrity and pay your bills unless you have a contract in writing absolving you of them from each creditor.

Successful raising of money occurs only through the pursuit of a deliberate and carefully planned, multifaceted strategy. The most financially sound nonprofits have a comprehensive fund development plan, which usually includes a variety of methods for raising money over a twelve-month period or fiscal year. Although churches are nonprofit organizations, they are not good models for resource development. A church usually gets most of its income from members' tithes and offerings. It may also receive some planned giving money from deceased members' estates. But by and large, the only time a church engages in substantial fundraising is for a capital campaign, when a new facility or capital expansion is needed.

We'll take a look at the most widely used methods of fundraising for grassroots and start-up organizations, and you can decide which will best fit your situation. A good approach for start-up projects is to try two or three methods in your first year. Branch out in subsequent years, once you have a bit of capital in your treasury. Be sure to check with an accountant regarding IRS guidelines for regulations and reporting of funds collected. Exhibit 4.2 gives an idea of the types of sources to consider in your development plan. Note that your organizational development plan is for the eyes of the board and staff only. It is an outline of where funding will be sought. You may find it useful to assign responsibility by name in each funding category. That way everyone knows who is responsible for which prospective donor relationship. Corporate and foundation sponsors should be identified by name, with an "ask" amount listed and a contact person on both sides of the relationship.

Each relationship should also be tracked according to how things are progressing. Don't assume you'll hit the jackpot just because your board secretary's brother-in-law is a corporate counsel for a major corporation. Although that relationship is a definite advantage, it is rare for one individual to have complete jurisdiction over any charitable giving program. Expect to realize your development plan goals over a long period of time. List realistic contributions based on current relationships, but project larger amounts as those relationships deepen and grow.

Notice that the first item on the example gift chart or development plan is board giving. It is generally assumed in the field of charitable giving that the person asking

Exhibit 4.2
Proposed Fund Development Plan

Gift Chart, 2006

Donor	Gifts	Total
Board members	10 @ $4,000	$40,000
Government agencies	Town: $5,000	
	NEA: $10,000	
	State: $30,000	$45,000
Corporate sponsors	8 @ $20,000	$160,000
Foundations	3 @ $8,000	$24,000
Individuals	100 @ $1,000	$100,000
Grand total for 2006		$369,000

Note: Does not include funds raised through entrepreneurial means.

for a gift has been among the first to give. Larger nonprofits have specific giving expectations, sometimes written in the bylaws and sometimes communicated in other ways. A young organization should not expect board contributions to match those of the Ford Foundation, but it should expect an amount that demonstrates a solid commitment as agreed on by the entire board. There is ample credibility in putting one's money where one's mouth is!

Raising Funds from Individuals

The *annual fund drive* is the most common and most relaxed way to fill your coffers. It is also the most lucrative. Approximately 70 percent of all funds raised come in the form of $25 donations from individuals who have a personal connection to an organization. In a start-up organization, the percentage is closer to 85 percent. These figures underscore the importance of the "personal ask" and the gospel truth of nonprofit fundraising: "People don't give to organizations; they give to people."

This approach usually lasts three to six weeks and then it's over. Individual donations are usually sought by board members, staff members, family members, relatives, client families, and others who have a close attachment to the work you do. Those small but consistent gifts are your fundraising bread and butter. Never discount their significance.

Federated Fundraising Efforts

This type of fundraising is defined by workplace drives, such as the United Way, the Junior League, or corporate giving programs. Many large companies allow and even sponsor this type of drive to demonstrate their support of the community. In this method, donors may designate which charitable organization they want the contribution to go to, whether that organization is a member of the federated entity's group or not. Sometimes the federated entity will retain a processing fee or a small percentage of the donation to cover its cost of administering the fund drive. You should ask that question before donating through any federated effort. Generally, as long as your organization has tax-exempt 501(c)(3) status, you may be included in federated drives. You simply have to inform your donors to clearly identify your program as the recipient of their donation.

Foundation Grants

As attractive as foundation support might appear at first glance, it accounts for only 5 to 10 percent of most nonprofit income. The best way to educate yourself about foundation grants is to visit their Web sites. Search on keywords such as *abstinence education, youth, health care, violence prevention, homelessness, job training,* and *prisoner reentry,* or go to www.guidestar.com to view 990 tax forms, which reveal the overall budget of a foundation and how much it gave away the previous year. Some resources that list foundations that give to religious and faith-based organizations are mentioned on our Web site, www.josseybass.com/go/esau.

Foundations have very specific giving guidelines. They will tell you what they give to, when and where their funding is available, and to whom they have given in the past. The application process varies from a two-page letter of inquiry to a full-fledged thirty-page proposal, depending on the size and scope of the foundation. Personal relationships are a contributing factor in foundation giving. It is common for a foundation representative to come for a site visit before committing funds. Be sure to do your homework and ask for an amount that is within the foundation's normal reach, and pay close attention to its areas of funding. For example, don't ask a foundation to give to your teen twelve-step program if it gives only to environmental conservation causes. An example of a request to a foundation is presented in Exhibit 4.3.

Corporate and Business Giving Programs

Corporate and business giving is a growing source of funding for nonprofits. It used to be that only the largest companies, such as General Electric, Ford Motor Company, Procter & Gamble, and Johnson & Johnson, set aside funds for charitable giving. Today, an increasing number of small businesses are doing the same on a smaller scale. It is worth checking out the companies in your area to see which have charitable giving programs. Sometimes it is not a formal practice, but if you have personal contacts, as with a CEO or a bank president, they may invite your organization to submit a proposal for a particular project that needs support.

Keep in mind while investigating this potential resource that businesses are interested in *win-win* investment opportunities. You will do yourself a favor if you present an opportunity for the company to gain recognition in the community, receive a well-publicized award for its help, or gain exposure by greeting your constituents at a communitywide event.

Again, do your homework; ask someone you know who works at the company you want to approach. Find out who the point person is in the giving department. Invite that person to coffee, and give that person your case statement or other promotional materials you might have. As with most fundraising, personal relationships are often the keys to success.

Letter of Inquiry

Another effective tool for attracting community, business, or local government support is the letter of inquiry (LOI) or initial proposal for support. This is a short document, usually between two and four pages long, outlining the project for which you are requesting support (see the example in Exhibit 4.4). It is concise and is considered a "first point of contact" with a funding source. The LOI takes language directly from your case statement and adapts it to the individual reader or business representative. One mistake young organizational leaders often make is not following up on all LOIs in circulation. Don't wait for funders to call you; allow a week or two, and call to see if they received your letter. Don't ask for money at that point; suggest meeting to discuss your work in greater detail to see if there is a way you can work together to accomplish one another's goals in the community.

Exhibit 4.3
Sample Letter Requesting Funding from a Charitable Foundation

Faith Training Institute
851 West James Street
Richmond, VA 23218
May 28, 2005

Charitable Foundation
771 Eighth Street
Cincinnati, OH 45202

Dear Ms. Jones,

I read the profile of your foundation in the *Christian Directory of Foundations* and would like to receive any guidelines or application materials you could send.

The Faith Training Institute (FTI) exists to "develop and share resources and train social entrepreneurs in best practices to increase the effectiveness of faith-based organizations around the greater Richmond area." It was incorporated in response to the Faith-Based and Community Initiative by a team of professionals and volunteers with decades of experience and demonstrated commitment to Christian principles. We design and facilitate project partnerships that address the needs of both urban and rural communities, including substance abuse, homelessness, food distribution, emergency response, education, and transitional housing. Our partnerships are guided by Christian principles and management, which ensures our common values.

Many new government opportunities to serve communities in need are opening up to faith-based organizations as a result of welfare reform and the recent Faith-Based Initiative. Our constituent organizations are preparing to answer the call by investing in tools and training that refine their work. FTI is supplying these resources to faithful servants through creative project design and grantwriting. The truth is, there are too many opportunities to pursue in our current understaffed condition. We need support for operating expenses, matching funds, and project management in order to take full advantage of all the available opportunities.

Thank you for your commitment to the Christian community and to our neighbors in need. We promise to conduct our work in a way that is pleasing first, to God; second, to the people we serve; and third, to our investors, who join us in fulfilling the Great Commission and Commandment.

I look forward to receiving your informational materials.

Sandra Elliman

Executive Director

Exhibit 4.4
Sample Letter of Inquiry (Initial Proposal for Support)

Emerald City Outreach Ministries

The first announcement of Emerald City Outreach Ministries' Capacity Building and Technical Training Institute will go out to seventy-five organizations over a twelve-mile radius. These organizations will cover a wide range of service areas across a continuum of care: homeless shelters, substance abuse treatment facilities and programs, transitional housing facilities, at-risk youth programs, before- and after-school child care programs, women's shelters, food distribution centers, parenting support programs, community technology centers, and more.

Of the initial seventy-five organizations, we expect to enroll fifty for the first round of instruction. These fifty organizations may send two staff members for training in the first round: one from management and one from direct service.

Exhibit 4.4
Sample Letter of Inquiry (Initial Proposal for Support), Cont'd.

Of the expected fifty organizations, we expect twenty-five to finish the first six courses of study. The coursework includes participation in four interactive training sessions. However, to be considered for the community regrant, it will be necessary only to complete four of the six courses of study within four months.

Project Purpose

To equip social service providers with capacity training to better meet the demands of a community in distress.

Goals

To breathe new life into a distressed community by addressing critical needs of the poor with immediate, effective services for lasting results.

Outcomes from the Initial Course Offerings

- Implement two new fundraising tools or strategies
- Develop a projected budget for each program in the agency
- Construct an agency logic model
- Apply for state certification (if applicable)
- Begin the accreditation process (if applicable)
- Write staff job descriptions
- Write board job descriptions
- Develop relationships with at least three other complementary service agencies

Community Outcomes Resulting from This Project

- Greater sense of community connection and participation in local events
- Increased community pride and ownership of issues
- Expanded services throughout the area
- Reduced crime due to more personal investment in the community

- Increased academic performance among students due to improved community identity
- Decline in teen pregnancy due to shared responsibility and concern of the adult population
- Reduced vagrancy due to increased community care projects
- Reduction in substance abuse due to shared community concern
- Reduction in jobless rate due to restored hope and new opportunities to serve
- New businesses established due to improved neighborhood attitude
- Reduction in poverty rate due to increased jobs and better business climate
- Increased home values due to elevated community profile
- Increased county tax revenue

Direct Mail

This method of raising funds is much less effective than it was twenty years ago. In our day of junk mail overload, most direct mail appeals are tossed out with the credit card offers and political appeals addressed to "Resident." That said, some of the larger organizations still conduct direct mail appeals during the holiday season when many people are still touched by a picture of a child receiving a wrapped gift from Angel Tree or the homeless man enjoying a hot turkey dinner.

Direct mail is expensive to produce. Normally, an organization will hire a public relations firm to produce the piece and then send it out to a target audience, expecting not more than about an 8 percent return on the investment. Not only must you pay for the design and production of the piece and postage to send it, but you will also have to pay for a list of addresses you may use only once. This method can cost anywhere from $10,000 to $50,000, depending on the scope of the mailing.

It isn't a practical method of raising funds for a grassroots organization because it takes so much up-front money to realize a very small gain. But if you can get some of this work donated (for example, design or printing free of charge), it may be something you want to consider.

Phonathons

Like direct mail, the telephone contact (or "cold calling") method was more effective in the past. With Caller ID and solicitation blocks on telephones, the phonathon method has been reduced to an exercise in frustration. You are better off approaching people in person and leaving the telemarketing to universities and firefighters' associations or working off a "warm" list of alumni or previous lapsed donors.

E-Marketing and Internet Advertising

Obviously, the Internet is the tool of the century, not just for corporate America, but for us as well. Tremendous results can come from using the Internet effectively, but you are best off finding an expert to handle this project for you.

Some companies exist that for a nominal fee will create for you a Web site with an online giving component and a monthly e-appeal that goes out to whomever you want to add to the list. The site can also track the number of recipients who open your message and give you a demographic breakdown of where your appeal is most successful. One group I have worked with for several years is www.brandinthebox.com, a cutting-edge group of professionals who will tailor your strategy to your strengths and needs. They are faith-based but work with secular businesses and nonprofits as well. Their specialty is grassroots groups operating on a tight budget.

Don't discount the many college students today who have tremendous expertise in the realm of cybermarketing. A great source of cutting-edge talent is found in community college technology departments. You can find a student who is earning money to put toward a university education by performing small contracts, such as building Web sites for smaller nonprofit organizations. Contact your local community college technology department head, and ask for some referrals.

Government Grants

This matter is addressed in great detail in Chapter Six. Since many readers of this book are primarily interested in new opportunities and government grants for faith-based organizations, I must warn you that the government granting process is arduous. If, after reading up on the ins and outs in Chapter Six, you still want to pursue that tack, *go for it!* Keep in mind that the turnaround time for federal grants is three to twelve months from the award announcement. State grants may not take that long, but many states have a biennial contract announcement system, meaning that if you miss this year's request for proposals, you may not have another chance for another two years.

County contracts are more realistic for grassroots organizations to pursue. They are often in smaller dollar amounts and issued for just a year at a time. But they are a great way to get your foot in the door to government funding. Often a state agency will consider a proposal from an organization that is already partnering with a county agency.

Don't discount the benefit of participating in a government grant as a subcontractor. This, too, is a great way to prove the success of your outcomes while operating as part of a larger whole. For example, you might be given a contract to provide summer academic and enrichment programs for at-risk youth as part of a Department of Education Twenty-First-Century Learning Center grant that your public school district acquired. Any partnership such as this will set you up for more significant funding later on.

Fundraising Events

You have probably attended some fun events in support of charitable organizations in your area. This approach is the best by far for attracting public awareness in the community. You can be assured that the better the event, the more work went into the planning. And most likely, the better the event, the more money it took to produce. Next to direct mail, events are the least cost-effective way to raise money. The reason is not that they don't bring in large amounts but rather that they cost so much initially.

Expect to lay out a minimum of 60 percent of the amount you hope to raise on mounting the event. That is conservative; large organizations are often willing to invest 70 percent to gain a 30 percent return. So if you are planning, say, an auction to raise funds for your operating budget, which is approximately $100,000, your event will have to bring in about $160,000. The line items to budget for are things like food or catering, entertainment, the auctioneer company, a professional fundraising or auction consultant, and procurement and collection expenses. It doesn't make sense to put so much effort into an event that will raise a mere $5,000. You could raise that by taking some key donors to coffee in a week's time.

But if your objective is to raise awareness about your work, an event is an excellent way to do that. Look into community activities, like Fourth of July parades or sidewalk sales at your local mall, or host a "Taste of the Town" by inviting chefs from local restaurants to contribute a dish and then having the public pay a flat fee to come and sample the food in a fun atmosphere. Plaster your program's name all over the brochures, napkins, signage, and other items, and as benefactor of the event, you collect the profit after expenses have been covered. If you include local press personalities, they will write favorable stories about you for weeks to come.

Church or Denominational Support

One of the huge advantages of being a faith-based program is that you have unique resources available that you probably didn't even consider. If you belong to a church that supports social ministry, you should begin your fundraising efforts there. Many churches have budgets for domestic missions, which refers to local or nearby social ministry performed by or through members or partners of their church. In my church, a significant amount of the domestic missions budget goes toward supporting an organization that provides school supplies, clothing, medical care, and other necessities for urban youth in our region.

Many large denominations and parachurch organizations, such as the Assemblies of God, Catholic Community Services, Lutheran Family Services, the Jewish Federation, and some Baptist conferences, along with many Presbyterian and Episcopalian churches, also welcome proposals from grassroots and faith-based organizations whose work matches their priority areas of service. These connections are also great partners for foundation or government grant proposals. A smart way to structure your partnership would be to use the large organization as a "fiscal agent," "fiduciary partner," or "lead applicant" in a project that would meet a local need. This partnership provides a grassroots or start-up program with a responsible partner with sound financial and governing mechanisms in place, which lend stability and sustainability to your proposal.

GIFTS IN KIND

As with most of the advice you have gleaned from this book, pray for an open heart and a creative mind to direct you in how best to find funding for your work. Perhaps the most creative way to help fund your project is through *in-kind contributions.* This refers to any type of support or donation other than money. And there are almost countless ways you can receive income through gifts in kind.

Have you ever given clothing to Goodwill? That is a gift in kind. Goodwill Industries began its work by distributing gently used clothing and appliances to folks who couldn't afford to buy those things new. Today, we hear appeals on the radio for "old cars, running or not!" which are collected by a nonprofit (or its agent) and sold through a variety of outlets. The profit is then collected by the charitable organization to fund whatever it chooses.

Hard goods are not the only way to receive in-kind support. Donated services are a great way to reduce your operating budget and establish a great relationship with a professional business. For example, asking a local print shop to print your brochures as an in-kind donation is common. Some homeless shelters enjoy the services of doctors and medical professionals as in-kind gifts on a rotating basis. Community legal foundations invite lawyers and judges to come in on a flexible schedule to help advise clients on legal matters that are beyond their ability to resolve. These professionals donate their time and expertise to help folks negotiate debts, settle housing matters, collect past child support, and even solve domestic violence issues.

You will read a sad story about donated office space in Chapter Five that illustrates an in-kind gift gone sour. It can happen to the disappointment of many. But never assume that it is impossible for anyone to donate services to your project. Instead, present your situation to someone you think might be interested in helping you, and then ask how he or she might be able to contribute. You will be surprised at the creative answers you get to that question.

Even the government gives useful items away—everything from food to office furniture and computer equipment to automobiles to housing—and they are given away at a fraction of the cost, if not for free. Most states' Web sites have a link where they list the items they want to sell or give away. You'll need to go first to your state's government Web site, such as www.ohio.gov. Look around or use the search option to find "general services" or "state administration." The page is probably tucked away deep in the recesses of some huge state department, but spend the time hunting—it's worth it. My state gives away computer equipment that is one to two years old to nonprofits. It also sells cars and trucks with only 30,000 miles for better prices than you could find on eBay. Government vehicles and equipment are usually very well maintained, so the risks are less than buying from a private citizen. Check it out!

RECOGNITION AND ACKNOWLEDGMENT

There is simply no way to thank your donors too much. Think back to your own experiences of giving to worthy causes. Didn't you look for that thank-you note in the mail after a couple of weeks? Most of us do. It is perhaps the most important point of contact you will have with your supporters. Thank them correctly, and they'll bring their friends along. Forget to say thanks, and they won't hang around for long.

Some professionals say that donors should be thanked five different ways: privately, publicly, verbally, in writing, and with a small gift. That might be a bit "old school" for the new millennium, but the concept holds true: *make a big deal about thanking donors.* Of course, when they give a million dollars, they expect a wing of the university to carry their name. But your situation is probably somewhat more modest. So how should you thank folks who give $25 and are the bread and butter of your income?

Here are some simple, inexpensive ways:

- Send a handwritten note from the director or the person who is most visible in your organization
- Publish a list naming all the donors (without mentioning the amount given) in a newsletter
- Highlight a specific donor once a month in an online newsletter
- Invite all donors to a casual lunch, and bring in a guest speaker to thank them
- Host an evening event at which you highlight a project that donors have paid for
- Take out an ad in the newspaper thanking all your donors, identified by name
- Post a plaque in your church or facility with donor names for each year

There is no limit to how you can thank your donors. It can be done quarterly or yearly. But each donor should at minimum receive a sincere letter with an original signature at the bottom. An e-mail isn't enough, nor is a general statement thanking "all of you who gave to our cause." Individual, personal thanks must be extended if you want to retain your donor base. *And you do,* because losing donors is inefficient and expensive to correct.

EARNED INCOME

One of the fastest and most effective ways of raising money today in the nonprofit realm is through earned income, also known as "entrepreneurial action." Churches are opening thrift stores. Food banks are hosting holiday boutiques selling fine handmade decorator items. Small private schools cut CDs of their choir and band performing Christmas carols and sell them to extended families. I know of an urban homeless shelter that obtained all the necessary permits from the city and the county health departments and opened a lunchtime sandwich delivery business. It is a thriving success!

Earned income, no matter how little money is earned in the beginning, is a huge benefit to all your other fundraising efforts. It demonstrates to a donor or investor that your organization is not just waiting for money to drop from the sky in order to make ends meet. You are pursuing creative avenues to supplement the funds that are donated to you in good faith. It clearly shows that you take your work seriously and are willing to do whatever it takes to make your organization a success.

Check with an accountant to ascertain just how much you are allowed to earn as a 501(c)(3) nonprofit. You may need to file as a new business, depending on the type of entrepreneurial venture you wish to attempt.

chapter
FIVE

Setting Up Shop

Location, Logistics, and Timing

The prospect of setting up shop raises a slew of questions: Do we need our own space? Where should we look? Can we afford it? Are we willing to work without a salary for a while? Who might donate space to us? Proceeding through these questions will bear fruit if you are honest and patient.

Believe it or not, setting up shop is often the most fun in the getting-up-and-running process. After all, now you're finally getting somewhere! You understand who you are or want to become, you know what you do and why you do it, and you know what it takes to become a full-fledged nonprofit and what it takes to run your organization. Now you are free to think about setting up shop.

This is a scary step for many people—it's really where the rubber meets the road. Physical space requires a budget, a plan, committed leadership, a client or constituent base to serve, insurance, and other hidden things you won't know about until you take the step to move into a facility. But don't lose heart: you have come this far because you answered your call. That call came from God, and you know He will complete it.

But how do you know if the time is right for you to take the plunge and move your operations into an actual physical location? The checklist presented as part of the following discussion will help you make that decision. Like the other lists in this book, this is only a guideline to help you. You may have special circumstances that make these guidelines unnecessary or suggest different ones—if so, do what you must do. If you have an invitation from an established organization or business to move in and get to work while your benefactor covers all cost and liability, that's great! However, such decisions for most start-up organizations are less clear-cut, so a little bit of self-analysis is a good investment of time.

ASSESSING YOUR FUNCTIONAL NEEDS

Now is the time to objectively look at your situation from many perspectives. Do you really need your own physical space? Too often the visionary of your group is ready to jump into a facility before basic structures are in place. Let me tell you a personal story.

A few years ago, my organization was just getting off the ground. We had established a good reputation as an intermediary in our region for capacity building and technical training for nonprofits. We had a small government contract to conduct conferences and workshops, and we had developed some relationships with key decision makers at the federal, state, and local levels. We were really taking off! We needed our own space to conduct our meetings and take our work to the next level.

So I went out and found an office building I thought would be a good location for the work we did. It was central, parking was available, and we could expand easily when the need presented itself. The best part was that the building was 75 percent vacant, which meant that the leasing agent would be willing to deal. After two months of investigation and negotiation, I was able to get our organization a commitment for month-to-month occupancy on forty thousand square feet of downtown office space free of charge as an in-kind donation (see Chapter Four for more on in-kind donations).

Of course, free is rarely truly free: the deal required us to pay for insurance, utilities, and parking. Now, if we had been established for a few years, with money in the bank, this would have been a sweet deal. The problem was, we didn't have anything—only a good, albeit young reputation and a generous landlord who wanted to write off his donation. Well, the parking turned out to be a small obstacle. I found a garage one block away that was willing to give us a ridiculous rate of $5 per day for anyone coming to our office. But the insurance and utilities on forty thousand square feet on the sixteenth floor of a nice office building was more than we could afford—about $1,200 per month.

After several disappointing meetings, our board decided it was too early to take advantage of this great opportunity. I had the tough job of relaying that information to the donor, who had put hours of work into making the idea viable. The worst part of the ordeal was the damage that the outcome wrought on our relationships. Though I always try to conduct myself in ways that will not damage a relationship if things don't work out, this experience did cost our organization a valuable friendship. It is important to learn from the negative experiences as well as the positive ones.

So let's look at your situation. Are you asking the right questions in anticipation of setting up shop?

You Know It's Time to Move If . . .

- Your working conditions have become so cramped and cluttered that you can't find anything
- Your children are answering your business line and not taking good messages
- Your meeting attendance has outgrown your local Starbucks
- You've overstayed your welcome at your current meeting place: home, church, or brother-in-law's warehouse
- The clients or public you serve can't easily get to you

In short, you know it's time to move if your facility is not able to keep up with the demands of your work.

If you have now determined that it is indeed time to find a better facility, location, or storefront, it's time to get serious about finances. Once you commit to a physical office, your responsibilities multiply, just as when you move from an apartment into a house of your own.

Let's assume that you're just beginning to work in your target population with a couple of services. Perhaps you and a few friends are volunteering in the local public school district with some computer training modules, or you teach English as a second language (ESL) in your neighborhood high school. Your system works well, and you have been asked to expand your work into the neighboring school districts with a small grant of $5,000. Is this an indication that you should find your own office space and take things to the next level? Do you really need your own space with a phone and fax, an expensive copier, and a four-color brochure?

Those things might be nice and might make your life easier, but they are also encumbrances that might cause you more anxiety than they're worth. Consider the following true example.

The board of an entrepreneurial urban church decided it was time to do something about the failing schools in its city. A couple of credentialed teachers who were members of the church approached the school district and offered an after-school tutoring program in two district high schools. The district was fairly positive about the idea but told the volunteers that they must have the approval of the individual principals in order to proceed. The principals were not excited about the "nice church people from the other side of town" coming in and fixing their problems. However, a very assertive PTA chairwoman got wind of the offer and welcomed the tutoring program into the school without consulting the principals. She told the volunteers they could move right into her PTA office and set up shop right in the midst of the faculty, students, and anyone else who walked the halls of the distressed school. When the PTA chairwoman went to the principal to explain the situation, she brought along about fifty parents. The principal was forced to concede and allow the program to go forward. Along with the agreement was a small grant for the start-up expenses that came directly from some of these low-income parents who desperately want their kids to get a good education.

This isn't an ideal way to start a school program. But it does teach us not to give up just because one individual is against us. We also see that financial support can come from surprising places. It also teaches us to find the real source of power in a situation and consult with that person before acquiescing.

If your situation is comparable to this example, here is what you might do. First, thank the donor of the grant and ask what the expectations are if you accept the gift or contract. As we already learned, donated money usually comes with strings attached—a designated purpose and often peripheral expectations that may or may not be written down. If the money is simply for you to continue doing what you are doing and just add in another school at your discretion, you have a lot of freedom to work. If, on the other hand, the grant comes with a list of cans and can'ts, you need to sit down with the appropriate person and hash out the details.

Assuming that you have complete discretion regarding how you are going to expand your work, I recommend that you approach the school district for some space through which you can manage your operations. It could be an empty broom closet or a classroom that is used only part of the day. It could be the corner of a counseling office or a temporary building out on the playground. Scout around, and ask questions of teachers with whom you have good rapport. Do some homework, and if you sense a good solution, create a win-win situation for the school. Promise to bring in doughnuts once a week for the faculty. Become the kind of partner that both faculty and administration like to have around. Offer one of your volunteers to answer the phones one hour a day. Remember to be respectful and receptive to your partner's concerns.

Once you know the right person to approach, try using phrases such as "We can't wait to get started on this new contract, but we're a bit cramped in our current office situation. What are the chances of snagging a corner around here with a desk, phone, and file cabinet?" or "We could run the program so much more efficiently if we could be in proximity to the students. Is there the possibility of finding some shared office space in the building?"

See what I mean? It doesn't cost you anything to go "hat in hand" to the person in charge. Just remember to be humble; you will always attract more bees with honey than with vinegar!

This solution saves you the cost of rent and utilities but probably not supplies and materials. If you are really good at convincing others of the value of your project, you might write up a cost analysis of the program and present it to the principal or superintendent in hopes of gaining in-kind support for materials as well. Show how much the students gain from your service, the progress they are making, the per-student dollar value your program offers, and the hope of improved test scores. Then ask if the district could help you shave off any of the supplies expenses from their storerooms.

Another important advantage of this sort of setup is the proximity you and your volunteers will have to the population you serve. Eventually, when you embark on a serious fundraising campaign, your donors will have more confidence in your program if your operations and management are located right in the community where you conduct your services. The perception is that you'll be more fully invested in the lives of the folks if you shop where they shop, play in the same park, and so on.

This kind of arrangement is a true partnership that most large, established organizations such as schools, hospitals, churches, and community service organizations will consider. The most significant item on their budget is salaried positions. If you can provide worker-hours and expertise through your staff and volunteers, you remove the largest restraint on their budget. Materials and utilities are things they pay for anyway.

Never forget this ancient piece of wisdom: "You don't have because you didn't ask."

FINDING TEMPORARY SPACE

Interpretations of the meaning of "temporary" vary widely. Technically, we are all here "temporarily." But in terms of workspace, you'll find many more options if you think "temporary." The concept opens up new dimensions and encourages you to think creatively but also requires that you be flexible. However, there is a tricky balance you'll need to master.

If you do find temporary space, you'll need to present your program as permanent and stable in every other way. Go overboard in creating the impression that your services are "here to stay." The reasons for this are credibility and fundraising. It will be much more difficult to attract support in the way of funding and volunteer and board participation if it appears that you are in the neighborhood for only a limited time—"until something better comes along." Diffuse this impression by looking for temporary space only in the neighborhood or vicinity of where you will conduct your services over the long term. That way, if and when you do move into larger or more suitable space two blocks away, you'll retain your identity and presence in the community. Folks will know they can count on you to be there even if you expand and grow.

Remember, it is essential that your physical presence be amid the folks you serve. Don't limit yourself to space in an organization of similar service, either. Figure out what you need in terms of space, equipment, access, parking, and so on. You might need to consider dividing up the direct service portion of your program in one space and administrative or office needs in another nearby location. Then get the word out that you're looking for space.

How many friends, relatives, or professional people do you know that might have an extra empty office at their place of business? Accountants, lawyers, and high-tech companies often have extra space due to personnel changes and downsizing. Just send the word out that you're looking for some space in their neck of the woods; ask if they know of anyone willing to consider such an arrangement.

Maybe you know of a midsize business that has moved into a new building and planned for growth. Sometimes a company will occupy a space much larger than currently required, planning to fill it in two years' time. Such a company might consider letting you use the space temporarily with the understanding that in twelve or eighteen months you must find another location. That's OK. Think of it as a transition toward your goal of having your own building. Just be sure you don't forget to work on the next transition before you have to pack up and go!

Remember the example of the big corporation that was willing to give me office space? The win for the corporation was the tax write-off. Suggest that the owner or decision maker with whom you are negotiating look into the tax implications of donating space to you. Your benefactor can figure out the value of the square footage that is available to donate, add in the cost of utilities and other expenses, and actually come out ahead by having you fill the empty space!

CHURCH FACILITIES

Many of you reading this book have already worked your program out of your church building. This can be a wonderful arrangement under the right conditions. (Remember Janie Jones from the start of this book?) In many cases, you presented your ideas for a social ministry to your church board members or staff, and they joined your vision. Or some of you may even be leading a program out of your church that was originally established by the governing board. Now it has grown into a viable 501(c)(3) independent from the church corporation.

Usually a church will allow a social or "side-door" ministry to function out of the facility free of charge with the understanding that the governance of the program remains with the church board. A church may also subsidize the ministry, paying for part-time staff and materials and insurance and even sponsoring fundraising events to support the ministry. As already mentioned, a church membership can be a source of excellent and reliable volunteer and in-kind support.

So if you have established a program or a social ministry outside of a church and hit a brick wall, perhaps you want to consider approaching a church to take on your project as a new side-door or neighborhood outreach ministry. Understand, of course, that in so doing, you must submit to the authority and governance of the church under its bylaws or terms of agreement, which should be signed by all parties. But this arrangement can solve many of your start-up problems. I'll list some benefits of a church partnership; then we'll look at a few warnings to protect against.

Five Benefits of Working in a Church Facility

- *Cost.* A church will often allow a program to be operated from the building without charging rent. It may even provide phone service, utilities, liability insurance, and some materials and clerical assistance.

- *Location.* Churches are often in a part of town with high visibility. If it is an older church, it could be in the heart of an established business or cultural district, which gives your program good exposure, good urban demographics, and public transportation. Or it could be in the suburbs with plenty of space, parking, and access to higher-net-worth individuals who invest in work like yours.
- *Staff and volunteer help.* Face it: it's easier to do your work with lots of help. Church folks can be the most self-sacrificing and dedicated helpers in the world. If your program is located inside a church, you may have a friendly arrangement with the staff for help with answering phones, making copies, word processing, setting up meetings, or cleaning up afterward. You may also enjoy Sunday worship or Wednesday night opportunities to share your success and appeal for volunteer help.
- *Credibility.* You may already know that it can be tough to establish a reputation and credibility if you're a young organization and function on your own. Operating under the perceived supervision and guidance of a church gives you automatic stability and structure that can take years to build independently.
- *Accountability.* Being part of a church family offers you accountability and protection from the many unforeseeable obstacles down the road. It also provides wise counsel in the way of board members and administrative and teaching staff right down the hall.

Four Drawbacks of Working in a Church Facility

- *Unrealistic expectations.* Unless your arrangement is clearly written down and acknowledged by all partners, misunderstandings can quickly develop. You thought the receptionist was taking your messages, only to find out you missed important calls during the first week. You serve the largest number of single-parent families on Saturdays, but the church building isn't always open on Saturday. You plan to use the fellowship hall for a family event on Friday night, but the middle school kids are there when you come to set up.
- *Budgets, fundraising, and commingling of accounts.* This should not be an issue with the strict accounting practices that churches are bound by law to observe. However, it does happen that money from a weekend car wash disappears or is unaccounted for on Monday morning. It is always best to keep your own set of books as a protection against potential money discrepancies. Ask the church to

set up a separate account for your program with a code number or series of numbers that can always be traced directly to your fundraising efforts and expenses. For example, you may ask the church bookkeeper to assign a three-digit number specifically for your work. Then everyone knows that whenever they see, for example, a 700 code in the budget or the monthly accounting statements, that dollar amount applies to your ministry.

- *Breech of relationship.* Sadly, relationships can become as strained in churches as everywhere else. Your program can be irreparably damaged if your host church relationships suffer. Review the discussion of protecting your relationships in the sections on board formation and volunteer management in Chapter Three. If you have a falling out with a friend, staff member, or volunteer at the church, you may find yourself without volunteers for next month's day care or after-school tutoring. Don't let anything become so important that it ruins your relationships, especially at church.
- *Limited exposure.* Just as there can be added exposure by working out of a church, there can also be a limiting effect. For example, if you work out of a Presbyterian church, you may not have many Baptists or Jews come to you for help. Preferences and perceptions vary, depending on the area you serve. This concern can be overcome with good marketing and relationship building, but just accept that some people will prejudge your program because of where you are located.

THE NEXT STEP

OK, let's suppose you have traveled this route, shared space, borrowed space, and outgrown all the temporary office situations I could describe. It really is time for you to have your own warehouse, storefront, clinic, school, or whatever might be the case. It's time to get serious and become established in your own facility. What comes next?

This is the time to reassess your plans. Call a series of meetings of your board, advisers, stakeholders, and clients (the people you serve). Dig out your previous plans, your projected budget for the next year, and your logic models which you will learn about in Chapter Eight. Objectively evaluate how closely you have come to realizing your goals and objectives up to this point. That exercise will help you decide if you are truly ready for a more permanent situation.

Don't get discouraged if you feel stuck in this spot for as long as a year. There is no substitute for planning and executing operations according to the plan. Looking back before you jump forward will only strengthen your future. If you have deviated from the original plans and mission that your core group agreed on, now is the time to decide whether you want to go in a new direction (which might seem natural) or return to the original plans from the start-up phase.

Either way, setting up your own shop will require changes and adjustments that will bring many challenges. It's vital that your operations be firm and strong before you transition to your own space. Many examples exist of great programs falling apart after they move into their own facility. Prepare your staff, volunteers, and constituents for the transition by warning them of the challenges ahead. Draw them an accurate picture of what to expect.

Encourage staff and volunteers to ask questions and vent their concerns before the final decisions are made. Invite them to offer solutions to tough situations that crop up. That way, they feel their opinions matter and their contribution to the organization is valuable. Your staff and volunteers will be less likely to abandon you during the transition if they believe you care what they think!

This type of move could be compared to moving out of a college dorm, where all your basic necessities are met by someone else, and into a new home, where nothing works without deliberate homeowner attention. Here the need for job descriptions becomes even more obvious. Who deals with the new landlord, who pays the utility bills, schedules site tours, raises operating funds, and on and on? Only now, if some facility issues fall through the cracks (and they will), there is no one to whom you can pass the buck!

HIDDEN COSTS

Don't you just hate going to buy an appliance or a car advertised at one price and learning when it comes time to pay that there are additional fees, taxes, and hidden costs attached to the item? The same is true with facility moves. Expect to be bombarded with "extra expenses" for the first year in a new facility. As recommended throughout this book, *ask lots of questions!*

Though it is true that nonprofits are tax-exempt organizations, that doesn't mean we don't pay for lots of things we didn't have to pay for in a borrowed or temporary space. These surprise costs include such things as licenses, use permits, increased liability insurance, and city sidewalk maintenance fees.

So how can you figure out what your true costs will be in a new space before you sign on the dotted line? Here are a few ways to figure that out:

- Find another business in the vicinity, and speak to the manager. Ask how much of the monthly expenses are taxes and what kinds of unexpected fees cropped up after the business moved in.
- Go to the city or county planning commission or housing authority, and ask someone to explain to you what you might not know about moving into the building you have selected.
- Call the state licensing agency responsible for your type of work, and ask for the regulations pertaining to your field. There may be more than one licensing entity whose approval you need—for example, the Department of Social Work, the Department of Health, the Fire Department, and perhaps others.
- Make an appointment with the director of an established organization that performs similar work. Ask what kinds of surprises you can expect when you make this transition.

All this homework can be entrusted to a resourceful volunteer. Be sure to choose someone who can think on his or her feet and can anticipate questions and theoretical situations well enough to ask pertinent questions. Instruct your envoy to take copious notes. You may need to refer to these conversations later if you are challenged or charged for something you weren't prepared for. Also, you should be building relationships with people in authoritative agencies in anticipation of needing an advocate there some day.

OTHER CONSIDERATIONS

Setting up shop entails a lot of small matters that are irritatingly important because they project your image to the community. They tell the world who you are at first glance—which is probably the most significant and indelible impression of all. Here are a few image-building matters that you'll want to pay close attention to.

- *Exterior appearance.* How you present yourself to the street determines how people perceive you. Even if you are in an old building in a "tired" part of town, you can still keep your windows washed. Your premises should be litter-free, and the sidewalk should be swept. Your parking lot can be tidy, even if there are potholes everywhere. If possible, apply a fresh coat of paint before you move in. Just painting the door and window frames can present a well-kept image.

- *Signage.* A well-managed program, even on a shoestring budget, should have a large, professionally printed sign out front. You can probably get one of these printed as an in-kind donation by asking a local print shop. Suggest that the shop put its name in the corner for extra advertising. Of course, all signage and printed matter must be error-free. If you print a lot of signage from your computer, remember that spell-checking software doesn't always catch incorrectly used words or grammatical errors. Ask someone with fresh, educated eyes to proofread anything in print that describes your organization—several times, if possible. Your hours of operation and program schedules should also appear on the front of your building; this is a promotional opportunity for potential walk-in clients.
- *Mission, vision, and values.* These statements should appear everywhere, in a concise, abbreviated form, including the front of the building or storefront awning, for example: "HARVEST TIME—Fresh Food for ALL Our Families!"

  Remember that these statements tell your story and invite interest as well as community support. A short paraphrase of one or each statement is best for your letterhead or signage. People driving by can catch a glimpse of your mission and make a mental note to stop in later.
- *Promotional materials.* Now that you have an address, you should have new printed materials featuring that address ready to hand out, send out, or distribute in public places. Take the time to collect several samples from other organizations so that you'll know what you like, what is effective, and what not to do with your brochures. There are many good models of promotional tools already in print. The best ones incorporate a self-mailer so that a person who sees it and likes what you do can simply enclose a check and drop it in the mail. Again, be sure to have many eyes proofread these documents before the final printing. You don't want to print five thousand copies of something and discover a spelling or calendar error a week later.
- *Phone.* What bugs you most when you call an office or other place of business? Isn't it the annoying electronic phone system that keeps offering you "options" to choose from? Nonprofit organizations have a very effective secret weapon that can minimize that phone problem: volunteers. Find a few reliable volunteers to handle your phones, and you'll help your operations tremendously. A

warm, well-trained voice will improve your image and save you lots of hang-ups from potential supporters.

- *Web site.* Nowadays, this detail is no longer optional. You must engage the community through the Internet. Consider your Web site as the best opportunity to get your message out. Yes, it will cost you something, but there are lots of talented students looking for projects on which to demonstrate their skill. Find one and work closely together to get a creative Web site at a fraction of the traditional cost. Be sure to include online giving so that you can receive contributions through your Web site. Use the resource list at www.josseybass.com/go/esau to read up on the powerful future of online giving.

I realize that these few seemingly minor matters can take a huge amount of time and attention. It's all part of setting up shop so that you can maximize your success. Don't short-change any of them. They will reward you greatly if done well. And don't think you have to reinvent the wheel in any of these areas. Find good help; meet with your local community college placement adviser and offer a student internship to help with the work. Or call a university professor or business and marketing teacher and ask for student help with one or more of these specific projects.

Present a win-win situation for the volunteer, donor, in-kind supporter, and yourself by creating a partnership where everyone involved is excited about the project and proud of the result. Be sure to pass around a lot of praise and credit so that the team will come back for the next job and new friends will observe the experience and want to join the next team.

Remember that your image is projected by what the public sees and experiences when introduced to your organization. A very large benefit that will develop out of these small details will be donors, supporters, and investors who want to become a part of the winning team you have created. Of course, increased investment will ultimately reach the folks you serve and help relieve some of the pain you are addressing every day.

As you grow, you may become eligible for foundation, corporate, and government grants. That process is the topic of the next chapter.

chapter
SIX

Partnering for a Purpose

Charitable Choice Laws and Government Funding

Partnership means different things to different people. In this chapter, we'll discuss partnership in some detail in terms of working in a complementary relationship with other organizations and with government. I'll explain the various levels of partnership and the levels of government funding, which influence the types and size of grants your organization may be eligible to receive in the future. I'll also introduce Charitable Choice laws that dictate how faith-based and community organizations may contract with government through the grant process.

I realize that many of you are reading this book for this one chapter alone. Actually, the concept of government–faith-based partnership is what created the demand for this book over the past few years. To be sure, I can only offer an overview of the issue in this brief chapter. There is much more information available at the links provided on our Web site, wwwjosseybass.com/go/esau. But be encouraged by the fact that since the 1996 Welfare Reform Act, churches and faith-based social ministries have enjoyed increased cooperation from some significant government agencies, including the U.S. Agency for International Development (USAID) and the departments of Health and Human Services, Labor, Housing and Urban Development, Justice, Agriculture, and Education. The foremost authority on this subject, Dr. Stanley Carlson-Thies, who wrote the foreword for this book, has published most of the related material since 1996. He was appointed to the White

House Office of Faith-Based and Community Initiatives in 2001 and is currently a senior fellow at the Center for Public Justice. Dr. Carlson-Thies is a dear friend of mine and allowed us to reproduce much of his work in this chapter and in the resources at the back of this book.

Note that there is no new or special money available for faith-based organizations or churches that conduct social ministry. The Charitable Choice laws that are in place do not provide set-aside funding for our work. They simply remove discriminatory hindrances and barriers that faith-based groups had traditionally experienced. A major source of resistance to the Faith-Based Initiative is other recipients of government contracts, who see us as new competition for the funds they now receive.

When I am asked by ministers and service providers, "How can I get some of that new government money set aside for churches?" I have to sigh and gently explain how the system works. The door to government contracting with people and organizations that operate from a philosophy of faith, once firmly shut in many places, is opening up a bit. We now have the same opportunity to compete and apply for funding as the other programs that currently have contracts. We must dig through the mountain of information flowing from the government and jump through the same hoops as all those other organizations that have been filling out grant proposals for years.

No preference is given to faith-based providers. Occasionally you may see an announcement for funding that includes a phrase like "especially encouraged to apply are faith-based organizations . . ." but this does not imply that those groups will be given preference over others. It just means that the agencies are trying to interest newcomers to the realm of serving the poor who formerly assumed that they were ineligible for such funding.

The original intent of the 2001 executive orders establishing the Faith-Based and Community Initiative was to "level the playing field" for faith-based and community organizations to submit proposals for contracts and grants for the social services they provide in their communities (see Exhibit 6.1). The rationale for both welfare reform and the Faith-Based Initiative was the reality that the Great Society of the 1960s had not achieved its goals of eliminating poverty, and forty years of government solutions toward that end had only exacerbated the situation. The Faith-Based and Community Initiative is an attempt to correct that course.

Thankfully, federal officials have realized that many government policies regarding social service grants and contracting have excluded smaller, conviction-based groups that do much effective work at the neighborhood level. Since welfare reform, the reallocation of community services block grant programs, and

Substance Abuse and Mental Health Services Administration adjustments, the federal government has crafted "equal treatment" rules that apply to all other federal funds. Keep in mind it takes time for the federal mandates to be implemented at the state and county levels, which is where most of the available money is distributed. Some states, like Texas, Colorado, Virginia, and Alaska, have done quite well adjusting their state practices to comply with the federal laws. They have even established their state Office of Faith-Based and Community Initiatives. But as at the federal level, these offices have no funds to administer. They simply act as information clearinghouses to help people like you understand how the system works.

Other states are in serious violation and have been since 1996. Of course, if you live in a state where the granting and contracting policies have not kept pace with the federal government, you will be frustrated and wonder why your grant applications are repeatedly declined.

According to Dr. Stanley Carlson-Thies, the Faith-Based and Community Initiative is really just "a redesign of how government works." It is an acknowledgment that effective, lasting solutions to the social problems all across America can often be found in places of worship or refuge, such as a residential substance abuse clinic or a homeless shelter sponsored by a religious denomination. In fact, personnel of these facilities are increasingly recognized as "experts in the field" due to the longevity of their service and the positive results they often accomplish.

Though thousands of heartwarming stories circulate about the changed lives that occur in faith-based social ministries, very little scientific research exists to support the claim that faith-based programs are more effective and get better results than most traditional government-sponsored programs. However, more and more data become available every year. Some pending research is listed on our Web site, www.josseybass.com/go/esau. Some of the completed studies indicate that faith-based programs can be more successful than secular and government-sponsored programs; others find no significant difference. Although results vary, depending on the study design and the data collection methodology, note that no study so far has shown that faith-based programs are *less* successful than any others.

For the purposes of this book, let's concentrate on the issues surrounding partnerships between government entities and faith-based social ministries, whether church-based or independent. Resource C contains a great selection of frequently asked questions and answers to them. They should help you decide how you wish to use the information given here. And again, more in-depth resources are identified on our Web site.

Exhibit 6.1

Unlevel Playing Field: Barriers to Participation by Faith-Based and Community Organizations in Federal Social Service Programs (White House, August 2001)

- Only a small proportion of federal funds go to faith- and community-based organizations, although it is impossible to tell exactly what proportion.
- Most federal grant making does not have a strong performance focus or evaluative component.

Barriers to Faith-Based Organizations Seeking Federal Support

1. A Pervasive Suspicion about Faith-Based Organizations
2. Faith-Based Organizations Excluded from Funding
3. Excessive Restrictions on Religious Activities
4. Inappropriate Expansion of Religious Restrictions to New Programs
5. Denial of Faith-Based Organizations' Established Right to Take Religion into Account in Employment Decisions
6. Thwarting Charitable Choice: Congress' New Provision for Supporting Faith-Based Organizations

Barriers to Community-Based Organizations and Other Small and Newcomer Organizations

1. The Limited Accessibility of Federal Grants Information
2. The Heavy Weight of Regulations and Other Requirements
3. Requirements to Meet Before Applying for Support
4. The Complexity of Grant Applications and Grant Agreements
5. Questionable Favoritism for Faith-Based Organizations
6. An Improper Bias in Favor of Previous Grantees
7. An Inappropriate Requirement to Apply in Collaboration with Likely Competitors
8. Requiring Formal 501(c)(3) Status without Statutory Authority
9. Inadequate Attention to Faith-Based and Community Organizations in the Federal Grants Streamlining Process

Resources

Unlevel Playing Field: Barriers to Participation by Faith-Based and Community Organizations in Federal Social Service Programs (White House, August 2001); http://www.whitehouse.gov/news/releases/2001/08/20010816-3-report.pdf

Rallying the Armies of Compassion (White House, Jan. 2001); http://www.whitehouse.gov/news/reports/faithbased.pdf

The President's Management Agenda, Fiscal Year 2002 (Office of Management and Budget, August 2001), ch. 6: Faith-Based and Community Initiative; http://www.whitehouse.gov/omb/budget/fy2002/mgmt.pdf

Federal Grants Streamlining Program; http://www.financenet.gov/fed/cfo/grants/grants.htm

Legislation

Charity Aid, Recovery, and Empowerment (CARE) Act of 2002, introduced 2/8/2002 by Senator Joe Lieberman, co-sponsored by Senators Rick Santorum, Hillary Rodham Clinton, Evan Bayh, Jean Carnahan, Thad Cochran, Richard Lugar, Sam Brownback, Orrin Hatch, and Bill Nelson

Title I: Charitable Giving Incentives

Title II: Individual Development Accounts

Title III: Equal Treatment for Non-Governmental Providers

Title IV: 501(c)(3) EZ Pass

Title V: Compassion Capital Fund

Title VI: Social Services Block Grant

Title VII: Maternity Group Homes

For the bill text:

Go to http://thomas.loc.gov and enter S1924 in the "Bill Number" box under the legend "Search Bill Text 107th Congress (2001–2002)" at the top of the page.

For a statement by Senators Lieberman and Santorum supporting the CARE act, and for links to a summary of the bill and answers to common questions, go to http://www.senate.gov/~lieberman/press/02/02/2002207732.html

Source: Courtesy of Stanley W. Carlson-Thies.

WHAT TO EXPECT WHEN YOU APPLY FOR GOVERNMENT FUNDS

To set the stage for this topic, I think it's best to give you the negative news first. If you are coming to this opportunity full of expectations and inexperience, it's important that you understand the downside clearly before you approach the task of applying for government money. You will want to analyze every angle very carefully before you invest the time, effort, and money in crafting and submitting a proposal for a government contract of any sort. To learn why, read on. . . .

Partnership Defined

What accounts for all the recent fuss about the concept of "collaboration" or "partnership"? Five years ago, we almost never heard those terms applied to social services or ministry. It really all boils down to the emphasis placed on "outcomes," another frequently used term in our field. For decades, billions of dollars were being pumped into social services with almost no accountability or specific "outcomes" expected from the service organization. As long as the organization was delivering the services to the needy, very few checks were in place to establish if the work was indeed making an impact on society or resulting in the desired changes in people's lives.

Finally, the situation could be ignored no longer, and in 1996, Congress passed the Welfare Reform Act, which placed specific requirements on both the recipients of services and on the entities receiving government funding to deliver those services. For example, a five-year limitation was placed on certain benefits. Some welfare benefits were decreased for women who gave birth to children out of wedlock.

To incorporate the new standards, administrative changes therefore had to be made both on the government side and on the service delivery side. A glaring reality became clear: many programs and services were being duplicated in communities all over the country—an inefficient and unnecessary waste of service provider time and taxpayer money. The only logical decision was to trim the system and tighten up the requirements on all social services the government was sponsoring.

. . . Thus emerged the concept of collaboration or partnership. The theory is that similar or complementary service organizations can reduce waste, improve results, and save money by combining their efforts focused on one or two long-term outcomes. Another common concept in our field today is "wraparound services." Wraparound services are any extra activities that assist the client in achieving self-sufficiency. For example, a good wraparound service to add to a job training program would be child care. That way, a parent participating in the Temporary

Aid to Needy Families (TANF) program can take advantage of a free job training program and have her children cared for in the same building. Or the same job training program may offer free transportation to job interviews for all participants who complete the minimum training requirements.

Complementary services working in partnership for measurable outcomes is more successful for the client when wraparound services are offered. By working with similar programs toward a collective goal, accountability is built into the situation. Shared resources develop, and soon expectations for social change can rise realistically. When higher expectations are placed on the contract organization and the client simultaneously, the likelihood of ultimate success in achieving client self-sufficiency increases. This is now the stated goal for all folks using public assistance.

If the past forty years of our welfare system taught us anything, it is that giving people unlimited support without expecting anything from them in return only leads to generational welfare. This truth applies to both the recipients of that support and the people who deliver it.

Developing Ministry Partners

You will do yourself and the people you serve a great benefit by researching which other similar and complementary programs are functioning in your neck of the woods. Your funding proposals will be much stronger if you include these programs as neighbors and partners in your work. It doesn't need to be a formal partnership agreement. A simple verbal statement that you are finding ways to work together for a common goal goes a long way. Recent trends in social ministry emphasize the advantage of identifying "community assets" as you develop your partnerships. This is an extension of your SWOT analysis. Listing your communitywide assets, or positive neighborhood elements and features, will help you figure out whom you need to be in partnership with in order to achieve your goals in the most efficient way. Success often breeds success!

To develop some community partners that will strengthen your credibility and quality of service, simply make a list of potential groups you'd like to work with and invite them over for a brown-bag lunch. Or call them on the phone and ask if you could come for a visit to learn about what they do. Most nonprofits are honored to have visitors and complementary organizations interested in their work. This simple process will build a nice network for your organization and become the basis of a community partnership you can draw on as you seek to be more effective in your work.

Consider this example. An urban alternative high school meets in a church facility in downtown Houston. The school is administered by a retired high school principal who is also an elder in the host church. The school has helped forty-six students achieve their general equivalency diploma (GED) over the past four years. The teachers are all certified by the state and donate much of their "out of school" time promoting the school to potential donors.

This school could leverage its success greatly by approaching businesses and other community organizations for partnership in addressing the needs of these kids who drop out of traditional school environments. Here are some things the school might do:

1. Approach neighboring public high schools for use of their athletic facilities, art rooms, and music studios during times when they may be available
2. Invite local business leaders to come talk to the students about what it takes to work in their field of business
3. Visit the Department of Labor's One Stop programs to show students how to look for jobs, write résumés, and interview effectively
4. Invite a guest speaker from the Department of Justice to explain in detail the plight of incarcerated youth who don't finish their education
5. Ask a local university to provide social workers who need to accumulate intern hours to work with the school's students on a weekly basis

In pursuing such opportunities, the alternative school can develop substantial partnerships that will enhance its work and provide credibility throughout the community—all of which helps the school's eventual grant proposals tremendously. This process can be repeated over the spectrum of nonprofit work with little effort and significant results. As in so many other areas, the key is to *think creatively.*

THE DANGERS OF PARTNERING WITH GOVERNMENT

Let's be honest: certain aspects of the Faith-Based and Community Initiative raise red flags. And what exactly does "partnership with government" mean? It sounds like a cozy relationship—but is that really such a good thing? Let's put some of these questions on the table and give them a good going over. . . .

Red Flag 1: Government Usurping Your Authority

You must consider very carefully how your partnership with a government entity will affect the way you conduct your services. It is true that government contracts come with strings attached. Your job is to figure out how those strings will affect your work and if that particular contract is worth pursuing. For example, a government regulation might stipulate that all after-school tutoring programs under government contract must operate on a 2:1 ratio, meaning two students to one tutor at a time. If your program operates on a 4:1 ratio, you will be required to find more tutors to gain such a contract. This might put undue pressure on your operations when you aren't equipped for it. Before you know it, you're making lots of decisions based not on what is good for your constituents but rather on what the government agency wants you to do.

Or you may not have a formal reporting system in place for your program. You may be so hands-on that you haven't needed to go through the tedious exercise of filling out weekly forms and tally sheets. Most likely, you don't have the staff in place to do that kind of labor-intensive calculation. But all government and most foundation and corporate grants now require proof of your evaluation methods. This is actually a good thing that helps us determine if we are really accomplishing what we say we are. But it isn't easy to implement these systems. (We'll talk more about evaluation in Chapter Eight.) The more partners you have, the more complex your program evaluation becomes.

Partnering is really just a friendly term that conveys some type of working relationship. It can be as broad or as narrow as you and your "partner organization" are comfortable with. For example, you might offer parenting classes for teen parents at a local high school in the evenings. That high school becomes your "partner" in this program. Or you might offer the classes and circulate the news about your work through the juvenile justice department of your county government. The juvenile justice department can then be referred to as your partner, even though no financial arrangement is involved. Today, *partnership* is a buzzword that implies that you are well connected in your community. And it is virtually impossible to attract any government sponsorship if you do not have at least a few community partners. We will return to this topic later in this chapter.

There are other ways in which partnering with government diminishes your control over your work. It is your responsibility to ask lots of questions before you begin the long and expensive process of pursuing a government grant or contract.

Don't delude yourself into believing that if you do a good job providing your valuable service, the government entity will overlook or not enforce all the requirements listed in the contract. The grantors are bound by law to do so; you must comply, or several bad things will happen:

1. You will lose your contract.
2. Your constituents will be without service.
3. Your actions may put jobs in jeopardy.
4. You will give all faith-based providers a bad name.
5. All faith-based contracts will come under scrutiny.
6. You will tarnish the name of the Lord.

The following is a true story. A small faith-based service provider in one state did marvelous work and gained a contract with the state's social service department. At the time of the first reporting, it became known that the service organization was not in compliance with its insurance policy. The state agency warned the executive director to correct the situation within thirty days, or the contract would be at risk.

The organization was so small that its two employees were responsible for all the operations and couldn't stay on top of the compliance issues. They managed the matter quickly at the first warning. But the next quarter, the same problem arose. Again the state agency representative warned of the consequences of the noncompliance. This time it took a few months to correct the situation. The next quarter report listed the same problem, and so the state agency was forced to cancel the contract, lest it be in violation of its own code.

The cancellation of the contract meant that the thirty-five clients who were receiving help from a great organization were now left without their lifeline. The organization was not in a position to attract private funding to make up the contract dollars, so the program closed its doors. *Don't let this happen to you!*

Red Flag 2: Mission Drift Toward Government Dollars

How wonderful it sounds to have perhaps 50 percent of your budget provided under a reliable government contract—the money will just turn up regularly in your mailbox each month. What anxiety that scenario would relieve! Think about the changes and expansion those dollars would make possible. Think about the security and credibility your program would gain through such a partnership. All you have to do is tweak your mission statement to include a focus on "reentry of violent offenders" and you have a great shot at a huge state contract.

Guess what? It is never a good idea to alter your mission drastically to match the description of qualifications for any federal, state, or county grant. Drastic changes would be adding a service you have never performed before or implementing some project that doesn't have the unanimous and unflinching support of your board and staff. Sure, it is intoxicating to consider the effect that a sizable source of new funding would have on your operations, but if it would entail changing your core mission, the cost is too great. One or more of the following conditions will arise:

1. It will cause divisions on your board or among your staff. Unless there is total acceptance of the concept, potentially irreparable frustration, alienation, distrust, and hurt feelings may result. Trust your board and staff; you have welcomed them as advisers and coworkers. They have the best interest of the organization at heart.
2. Government grant reviewers and staff are very savvy in the field they are supporting. They will easily detect by reading through your proposal if you are trying to enter a field for which you are not sufficiently prepared. They see it all the time. You will have wasted a lot of time and effort drafting a proposal that will most likely be turned down.
3. You will be awarded and quickly rue the day you ever sought this contract. Adding a new focus area is not as simple as you might think in your state of euphoria. Most likely, too much of your time will be diverted to this new project, and the service for which you are best known will begin to suffer.
4. You may dilute your presence in your community by being stretched too thin. You won't continue to enjoy an excellent reputation because although you have added a service, you may not do anything very well. Your partner organizations may become confused about your priorities and abandon you.

These are a few warnings about seeking government dollars for work you aren't already doing well. One protective measure to put in place is a document adopted with guidelines and limits to what your organization will and will not do in seeking government funding. An example can be found in Resource D, "Government

Funding Policy: CityTeam Ministries." CityTeam Ministries has functioned well for almost thirty years in nine countries without government contracts. However, it is in a great position to partner with government in the area of homelessness and substance abuse treatment. Take a look in Resource D at how CityTeam handled the dilemma. And consider this: mission drift can occur just as easily if the big donor is a corporation, a foundation, or a private individual.

Red Flag 3: Separating Faith Components from Other Activities

Review the frequently asked questions in Resource C. Contracting with government entities means that you are agreeing to separate your religious component in time or location from the service the government is purchasing from you. For many faith-based social ministries, this just isn't possible. Teen Challenge, for example, would find it very hard to administer a federally sponsored abstinence education program minus its Christian message. But that is the fundamental issue at stake in government partnerships. Can you really deliver your service without evangelizing during your core teaching times and yet incorporate it in other parts of your program? Exhibit 6.2 details the firm guidelines of Charitable Choice.

Exhibit 6.2
Charitable Choice 101: An Introduction

Charitable Choice is a set of new rules that apply when a state or local government uses certain federal funds to buy social services. Past rules often required assistance to be secularized, and excluded many faith-based organizations from participating. Charitable Choice ensures that faith-based providers have a chance to compete to provide help and it protects their religious character if they accept government funds. At the same time, Charitable Choice protects the religious liberty of people needing help.

New Freedoms and Responsibilities

Charitable Choice:

- *encourages public officials* to obtain services from nongovernmental groups because community-based solutions can be key in fighting poverty and dependency.

- *requires government not to discriminate* against faith-based organizations when choosing contractors or deciding who can accept vouchers to provide services.
- *obligates government to respect the religious character* of faith-based providers that accept public money by affirming that:

  > they may display religious symbols and items,

  > they may use a faith-based approach and emphasize values and character,

  > they retain their right to use religious criteria in hiring.
- *protects the right of recipients* to be helped without religious coercion by ensuring that

  > they may not be discriminated against when seeking services,

  > they can decline to take part in inherently religious activities,

  > they have the right to an alternative if they object to a religious provider.
- *maintains the separation of church and state* by requiring that government funds be used only for the public purpose of assisting the needy, not for inherently religious activities such as worship, sectarian instruction, or proselytization. (Vouchers give clients more choices and impose fewer restrictions on providers.)

Constitutional Foundations

Charitable Choice rests on the constitutional concepts that government must not discriminate against religion when it selects service providers, may not endorse one religion or many, and must safeguard religious liberty for all.

Charitable Choice now governs federal (and admixed state) spending for:

> welfare services (TANF, in the federal welfare reform law, 1996);

> Welfare-to-Work program (adopted in 1997);

> Community Action Agencies (1998 reauthorization of Community Services Block Grants);

> SAMHSA drug treatment (Oct. 2000 and Dec. 2000 laws).

Exhibit 6.2
Charitable Choice 101: An Introduction, Cont'd.

Government Collaborating with Faith Communities

Government should work closely with faith-based and community groups. Government has great resources and can provide uniformity of service, while social organizations surround the needy, can better provide encouragement and challenge, offer connections to networks, and deal with moral and spiritual matters. Many kinds of cooperation are possible. Faith-based organizations can be encouraged to expand their own outreach to their neighbors. They can join a welfare department's referral system. Government and congregations can together build a mentoring network to support families.

In addition, government can purchase services from faith-based providers. Charitable Choice is not optional for any state, county, or city. It is the law of the land. Charitable Choice isn't a program to fund churches and synagogues. Instead it is a general principle that requires that faith-based organizations have a chance to compete for certain federal funds to provide services. Hurting people deserve the most effective help and now public officials can turn to faith-based groups along with other providers.

Making It Happen

Not all officials know about Charitable Choice or are complying with its new rules. Illegal barriers continue to be put in the way of expanded collaboration between government and the faith communities. Compliance is the first step forward.

Then the legacy of mistrust between many faith-based organizations and government needs to be overcome. Faith groups should take seriously the changed environment and explore the new opportunities. Public officials should acknowledge their need to become more hospitable to faith-based involvement and learn how to reach out. Government also can foster effective new collaborations by using smaller-scale contracts, encouraging subcontracting, and providing technical assistance.

A Challenge to Public Officials. For the sake of families that need extensive assistance and a community of care, give special attention to nurturing expanded relations with faith communities. It is not enough to say that the doors are open; constructive steps are essential to overcome the legacy of mistrust and to facilitate collaboration.

A Challenge to Conservative Faith Communities. Don't just say that serving the poor is the task of people of faith. Government officials recognize that public programs are insufficient and they want to collaborate with faith communities. The time to act is now. Take seriously government's offer with Charitable Choice to provide public funding without stripping religious organizations of the faith basis that makes them effective.

A Challenge to Progressive Faith Communities. Welfare reform needs further reform. Yet the needy also deserve to be reconnected to community and faith-based help. Advocate for policy change but don't neglect expanding your services. Take advantage of Charitable Choice to renew the spiritual depth of your services.

Resources

A Guide to Charitable Choice: The Rules of Section 104 of the 1996 Federal Welfare Law Governing State Cooperation with Faith-based Social-Service Providers (Center for Public Justice and Christian Legal Society, 1997); (410) 571-6300 or www.cpjustice.org.

S. Carlson-Thies and M. Rogers, "Charitable Choice: Two Views." *Sojourners*, July-Aug. 1998.

C. Esbeck, "The Neutral Treatment of Religion and Faith-Based Social Service Providers: Charitable Choice and Its Critics," in D. Davis and B. Hankins, eds., *Welfare Reform and Faith-Based Organizations* (Baylor University, 1999).

For extensive information on Charitable Choice, go to www.cpjustice.org.

Source: Used by permission of Stanley W. Carlson-Thies and the Center for Public Justice.

The reason for these guidelines is the protection of the client's rights, the protection of the religious character of the organization, and the protection of tax dollars. Government funds cannot be used to pay for Bibles or religious materials. Nor can those dollars be used to make repairs to the church roof, unless they are so designated. All religious activities must be conducted at times outside and separate from the purpose of the grant and may be offered to clients, but they may elect not to participate. Prayer, theological counseling, and spiritual guidance can still take place within the program. You just need to be more time-sensitive as to when these types of activities take place.

Here's how an acceptable program might look to the reader of a government grant proposal:

- You run a substance abuse twelve-step program three times per week.
- You are paid by the state to provide science-based treatment and counseling to addicts and people in recovery, and you must accept *anyone* who comes to you for help.
- Your proposal to the government agency does not include any budget expenses for "inherently religious materials" such as holy books or study guides featuring religious content.
- You begin each session with the singing of praises and worship, but program participants may opt not to join in.
- You then move into a time of prayer and personal meditation, which likewise must be completely voluntary.
- Then you break into small support groups or individual therapy, ensuring complete protection of information and privacy.
- You may not refer to specific religious content in your counseling or therapy sessions without the express permission of the client.

So, does your partnership opportunity still look inviting to you? If so, great—proceed with caution and an experienced adviser. The redeeming factor is that you may still conduct your services based on your principles of faith and even discuss matters of religion during times and activities that are not covered by government funding, such as mealtimes or personal mentoring sessions. There are many opportunities to refer to and incorporate your religious principles while you serve your clients. Continue to do good work from a heart of compassion, and they will be asking you for special times of prayer or contemplation. You just need to be more strategic in how you do those things if you receive government funding for your work.

For the most definitive information on these matters, refer to Exhibits 6.3 and 6.4, both by Stanley Carlson-Thies.

Exhibit 6.3
Charitable Choice: Top Ten Tips for Faith-Based Organizations

1. Plans, Not Just Visions. To be entrusted with public funds to serve the needy, you need specific plans for how you will help families overcome their problems. Faith is essential but no substitute for plans. Specify outcomes and demonstrate how your program will produce them.
2. Don't Chase Money. You have a right to compete for funding to provide services. Just be sure that the funds will help you carry out what you know how to do well. Don't be tempted to start a new program just because money is available for it.
3. Be Accountable. Make sure you have policies, procedures, and personnel that enable you to account for income and expenditures, monitor staff and volunteers, and keep track of clients' progress. Government will, and should, ask you to be accountable for how you spend, what you do, and what works.
4. Avoid Dependency. Never become dependent on any one source of income. Plan ahead what you will do if government funding dries up or an unacceptable condition becomes the price of continued funding. Establish a maximum percentage of funds from any single source.
5. Separate Incorporation. Establish a separate but faith-based 501(c)(3) corporation to receive government money and to operate your service programs. Your congregation will be protected from unwanted government rules and prying, and a separate structure can be specifically designed for effective services for the community.

Exhibit 6.3
Charitable Choice: Top Ten Tips for Faith-Based Organizations, Cont'd.

6. Join Hands. Your congregation has a vision for service? Wonderful. First step: see if any one else is already filling the need and join with them. If no one is yet active, get busy, but draw in others who share your vision and can bring their own expertise and connections.
7. Be Careful About Religion. Faith undergirds the solution. But the poor are not necessarily without faith; they may be suffering because of the evil of others. So let faith be resource, guide, and connecting point, not the end of the story. And respect, without ignoring, the alternative faiths many will bring.
8. Get into the Loop. Government contracting and policy making are long-standing operations with their own language, information channels, and players. Want to be serious about working with government? Find out what the loop is and get into it. Don't try it alone—join a network.
9. Check with a Lawyer. No matter how well you understand Charitable Choice, if you plan to get involved with government you first should consult with an attorney experienced with government rules and regulations, religious organizations, and the nonprofit sector.
10. Advocate as Well as Serve. As you serve the needy with your best efforts, don't forget that they may also need you to be on their side as their advocate to government. And don't let your focus on service blind you to the need for justice in public policies and economic life.

Source: Used by permission of Stanley W. Carlson-Thies and the Center for Public Justice.

Exhibit 6.4
What Difference Does Charitable Choice Make?

We'd like to award you federal funds so you can hire someone to train other churches to work as effectively as yours does in keeping teens out of gangs and juvenile detention, the mayor of the California city told the pastor. All you have to do is sign this form promising to ignore religion when hiring the new staffer, take down your religious posters and symbols, and run the program without any religious language or influence. Can I send you the money?

The pastor, of course, said No. Why expand a program if its soul first has to be ripped out?

But what should the pastor say if the government promises to respect, rather than threaten, the faith character of his program? There may still be reasons to reject the money, because collaborating with government requires great skill and particular capabilities and isn't for everyone. But there is good news. Congress is dramatically changing the rules so that officials can't demand secularism as the price for taking federal money.

Two Cheers for Charitable Choice

That dramatic change is called Charitable Choice. It is a new set of requirements that state and local governments must follow when they pay some kinds of federal funds to private groups to obtain services for poor and needy families. These new requirements are the opposite of the ones the California pastor confronted. According to Charitable Choice, a group receiving federal funds can display religious signs, does not have to suppress all talk of faith, and can choose employees based on their commitment to religious beliefs and action. Charitable Choice isn't a free-for-all. There are limits, of course. Providers may not force people needing help to listen to an evangelistic message or to pray and worship. Government funds can't be used to pay for holy scriptures or a chaplain. All clients have to be helped, even if they reject religion. Groups have to keep scrupulous account of government funds and comply with reporting requirements. (The government itself has to provide a secular alternative if a person doesn't want to be helped by a faith-based program.)

Exhibit 6.4
What Difference Does Charitable Choice Make?, Cont'd.

Does your program fit within these requirements? If religious elements are woven through in such a way that a person cannot get help without taking part in religious study, or if you require folks to pray or listen to holy scripture before learning how to search for jobs, then your program won't fit, despite the changes. But maybe it can be reconfigured without loss so that the inherently religious activities are separate and voluntary. Under Charitable Choice, faith doesn't need to be chased out of an organization, but religious observance can't be forced. Religious groups must think carefully about these and other rules before competing for funds covered by Charitable Choice.

So this is not a federal program to buy religion for the poor, and the new requirements are not as flexible as some groups would like. But Charitable Choice goes a very long way to make government's rules for buying services hospitable instead of hostile to faith-based groups.

Charitable Choice applies only to a few federal programs: Temporary Assistance for Needy Families (TANF), which replaced AFDC; the Welfare-to-Work program for hard-to-employ welfare recipients; Community Services Block Grants, which fund Community Action Agencies to serve low-income neighborhoods; and some drug treatment money (SAMHSA funds). That means that much, even most, federal money that is used to buy services follows other rules, rules that are very restrictive about religion.

One Cheer for HUD

The federal Department of Housing and Urban Development (HUD) has worked hard to build positive relations with houses of worship and faith-based nonprofits. HUD realizes that it must work better with religious groups that do so much to provide housing and other assistance for the needy.

So HUD simplified the process of applying for its grants. And it built a bridge to the faith communities with a special Center for Community and Interfaith Partnership to provide information and technical assistance, helping faith groups navigate a complex bureaucracy. So one cheer for HUD. But only one. Because although it laid out the welcome mat for faith-based groups, its rules for collaborating remain the old restrictive ones and not the new Charitable Choice requirements. In fact, the mayor in the story was simply telling the pastor about HUD's secularizing conditions for much of its federal money. It isn't all HUD's fault that it welcomes religious groups with one hand and enforces secularizing requirements with the other. The main problem is that Congress hasn't written liberating new laws for housing and community development spending. Congress passed Charitable Choice rules for other federal funds, but not for money HUD controls.

No Cheers for Most States

There is another problem. Charitable Choice is a federal provision that is effective in practice only when state and local governments modify their own contracting rules to bring them into line with the new federal requirements. Until they do that, officials will be as restrictive now as always when they consider who can get funds and under what conditions.

The sad reality in most states today is that although they have warmed up to faith-based programs, the rules on their books still are secularizing. Most states still tell providers that they cannot take religion into account in hiring staff, despite Charitable Choice. And some states still won't let so-called pervasively sectarian groups even apply for government funds.

The Center for Public Justice in September 2000 released a Report Card on Charitable Choice compliance that gave F's to 38 states. Only four got A's: Indiana, Ohio, Texas, and Wisconsin.

What Can You Do?

If you are located in a place that is ignoring Charitable Choice, don't be discouraged and don't give up. Some officials are just ignorant, so educate them. You may need to be persistent, asking around until you find an official who knows what the law now requires and who is eager to collaborate with faith communities. Talk to your state or federal elected representatives about Charitable Choice and ask why you are running into resistance. And you may need to talk with a lawyer who can remind officials what they are supposed to do.

Exhibit 6.4
What Difference Does Charitable Choice Make?, Cont'd.

Of course, if the funding you seek isn't covered by Charitable Choice, then you'll just have to work patiently and persistently to see how flexible officials can be as you demonstrate the effectiveness of your programs. And don't neglect to tell your members of Congress that you'd like to see Charitable Choice extended across the board.

In the meantime, even without any funds changing hands, you may want to collaborate with government so that you can offer your services to folks in the government programs. Or you might be able to work out a respectful subcontracting arrangement with a religious group like the Salvation Army, Lutheran Social Services, Jewish Federations, or Catholic Charities. They work well with government and sometimes want to connect more closely with congregations and grassroots groups.

New Administration Promises Changes

Shortly after taking office, President George W. Bush, as he promised on the campaign trail, announced he was creating a White House Office of Faith-Based and Community Initiatives to press the federal government to become as friendly as possible to religious and grassroots groups. He'll ask Congress to expand Charitable Choice to all federal social spending and have federal departments work with their state and local government partners to put Charitable Choice into practice.

Shine like Stars

Never let government money (or funds from a big donor, a corporation, or a foundation) divert you from faithful service to the needy. If the conditions aren't right, trust God to supply funds some other way. And wherever the funds come from, be sure to provide the most effective service possible. Show full respect for those you help as people made in the image of God, with inherent dignity no matter what their beliefs are. And handle funds with care; you are accountable to God, for sure, but also to everyone who helps to pay for your program. Believers should do everything with such integrity that even those who despise religion will acknowledge that you shine like stars in the universe as you provide assistance (Philippians 2:14–16).

* * *

Charitable Choice isn't perfect. But ask yourself: if your faith-based program takes government funds and you are hauled before an official who demands that you ban all religious influences and ignore the beliefs of new staff, wouldn't you rather have Charitable Choice to back *you* up and make *him* back off, instead of being subject to a law that says *he* is right and *you* must give way?

Although most states aren't complying fully with Charitable Choice, many now welcome collaboration with faith-based programs. As Amy Sherman shows, officials know that Congress gave a green light to collaboration, so they tend to be more flexible. But contracting requirements may be too restrictive. Consult a lawyer!

Amy's report is *The Growing Impact of Charitable Choice: A Catalogue of New Collaborations Between Government and Faith-Based Organizations in Nine States* (Center for Public Justice, March 2000). For more information, go to www.cpjustice.org.

Source: Used by permission of Stanley W. Carlson-Thies and the Center for Public Justice.

Red Flag 4: Potential Legal Action

It may sound crazy to think that you might be hit with a lawsuit just for offering a wonderful and needed service to the poor. But in the current climate of activist judges and confrontational watchdogs, it is a glaring reality. In fact, there are well-funded organizations prowling around like hungry lions just searching for faith-based organizations to "misstep" so they can claim discrimination or unfair treatment or mishandling of funds.

Again, I don't give you this information to discourage you. But you must go into a government, or any other partnership, with the whole truth. You who serve the One Who Called You understand that when you offer a cup of cold water in His name, you wear a target for opposition to strike. This situation may not continue forever, but for now, we have to work with what we know to be true; and in this case, *expect opposition.*

That said, there are several cases pending that may settle some of these issues in the next year. Pray that the results favor the folks who need your help and don't lead to a plethora of legalistic appeals that deny us the freedom to meet their needs under the new guidelines.

The good news is that many concerned, reputable lawyers are preparing even now to accept such cases as they arise, on a pro bono basis or at a greatly reduced rate. The Alliance Defense Fund, out of Arizona, has already begun developing a referral process for faith-based groups that might need legal help. Individual attorneys and law firms across the land anticipate the reality that the fate of the Faith-Based and Community Initiative could very likely be determined in the courts. Until then, it is vitally important that faith-based social ministries participate in the process on some level to establish credibility and precedence for such legal battles.

Red Flag 5: What the Future Holds

My assessment of the situation is very upbeat, especially after the reelection of President Bush. The new Congress seems to be more sympathetic and open to welcoming faith-based and community service providers into the family of social service partners. After meeting and working with many different government representatives from federal agencies to state bureaucrats, I have come to the conclusion that this trend toward faith-based–government partnerships will continue for quite a while. The reasons are as follows:

1. Government agencies are having a positive experience so far, for the most part. Staffers I have interviewed have said that the faith-based service providers are experts in their fields of service and willing to do whatever it takes to heal the wounds of the poor. They don't lock the door and pull down the shades at 5 P.M. every day.
2. Faith-based service providers have proved themselves to be polite, respectful, professional, and easy to work with. Those that have contracted truly want to comply and abide by the guidelines because it means serving so many more folks in need.

3. Faith-based volunteers donate hours far in excess of members of other demographic groups. Faith-based organizations have a seemingly never-ending supply of committed volunteers to help out, which keeps costs down considerably.
4. Accountability functions best in faith-based services where help is given by others in the immediate community. Follow-up and checking in occur on a daily basis instead of weekly or monthly. Relationships are long-standing and solid, leading to greater honesty and accountability. Families are aware of and involved in the troubled person's affairs and efforts at improvement.
5. Experience has taught us that the attempt to solve society's problems through government alone has not worked. The Lyndon Johnson's Great Society cost American taxpayers trillions of dollars and resulted in generational welfare, fatherless households, runaway substance abuse, and skyrocketing out-of-wedlock birthrates. Finally, in 1996, Congress had the courage to admit that the solution might best be found at the local, neighborhood level: hence the Faith-Based and Community Initiative.
6. Our government can no longer afford to take care of the poor and needy the way it has in the past. Owing to the rising costs of medical care, the huge immigrant population needing subsistence, and other contributing factors, it is simply impossible for the government to be all things to all people. The church is the best partner the government has in solving social problems.
7. Charitable Choice became law four different times under President Clinton. Federally funded child care has been occurring in churches since 1990. Supreme Court decisions have upheld the equal opportunity concept several times over many decades. The 2001 Faith-Based and Community Initiative isn't new; it's just a speedier implementation of what would have happened through another administration in perhaps another dozen years.

America is a very compassionate country. Americans see a need and jump in to meet it. That is the American way. Government will never back out of the process, nor should it. Rather, government should create a climate where people at the local level who are called to meet their community needs may do so without cumbersome government regulations and intrusions. If faith-based social ministry can steward this opportunity well, we just might see that ideal played out!

Personally, I believe that we who are called by faith to meet the tangible needs of the poor among us have a responsibility to respond and answer the call to the extent we are able. I believe that it is a matter of *stewardship* to answer the clarion and exercise our option while the option is still open. If we don't, we prove that faith-based social ministry is neither able nor interested in partnering with government to leverage our efforts in response to the needs of the poor and afflicted. If the faith-based sector as a whole declines the opportunity, we may see it close very soon. We need to ask ourselves, "What is the message we should be sending the world regarding this opportunity?" (For clear, up-to-the-minute information on the world of faith-based–government partnership, visit the Center for Public Justice at www.cpjustice.org.)

So how do you take advantage of the opportunity?

WELCOME TO "GOVERNMENT GRANTS 101"!

There are traditionally four kinds of funding entities that give money to nonprofit organizations: private and public foundations, corporations, government agencies, and the general public. All of these except government agencies are covered in Chapter Four on fundraising. So the rest of this chapter will focus on introducing you to government funding opportunities, which exist on four levels: the federal, state, county, and local or community level.

Federal Government Grants and Contracts

The federal government agencies announce grants, contracts, and partner opportunities throughout the year in a variety of ways and places. Billions of dollars are contracted out to nonprofit organizations every year, in the states and overseas as well. The most comprehensive listing of federal grants is found in the *Federal Register.* You may download anything from the *Federal Register* at www.federalregister.gov, but I don't recommend that route. The register is very difficult to read, full of legalese and references to other government documents and laws, and written in very small print!

The better way to access federal grant information is through the individual agency that handles your particular field of service. To date, the cabinet agencies that are participating in the Faith-Based and Community Initiative, as noted earlier, are USAID and the departments of Labor, Agriculture, Education, Health and

Human Services, Justice, and Housing and Urban Development. But don't assume that other government entities are off the compliance hook. All federal agencies should be working with FBOs on an equal footing. Surprisingly, the participating federal agencies are very willing and interested in helping newcomers to the field of government partnerships. In fact, sometimes, special consideration is given to grant applicants who have never received government support. Each of the departments has a small staff in its newly established Office of Faith-Based and Community Initiatives. They stand ready to answer your phone calls and e-mails promptly.

Make a note of any conference calls or "bidders' conferences" that are offered for prospective applicants. These meetings are a great way for the novice grantwriter to ask and get answers to absolutely any question. You will discover who your competition is and may even make a decision not to apply once you know how much or how little is available specifically for "new programs."

So if you intend to serve youth in the juvenile justice system, you would go to the Web site of the Department of Justice or call your regional Justice office for a "notice of funding availability" (NOFA). You can find agency Web addresses at our site, www.josseybass.com/go/esau, or just do a search using the department name and click on "funding opportunities," "RFPs," or a similar option.

Perhaps the most encouraging thing to happen for social ministry in the past three years is the formation of the Compassion Capital Fund (CCF) grants. This is an amount of funding administered through the Department of Health and Human Services (HHS) targeting faith-based and community organizations (FBOs and CBOs) that are in a position to help build capacity in other similar or smaller organizations. This idea encourages more intentional collaboration and partnership among FBOs and CBOs and welcomes more grassroots organizations into the family of social service delivery.

"Capacity building" refers to improving organizational infrastructure and systems, which allows for better, more efficient service to be performed. As more and more government contracts are established with community-level service providers, it is clear that most of these providers lack sophisticated systems to fulfill the requirements of government grant reporting. As we, a collective group of faith-based social ministry leaders, build our capacity and improve our systems of service delivery, our reputation and reliability for meeting community needs will increase, placing us in a much better position to attract a wider range of funders to our work.

The first Compassion Capital Fund total distributed amount was about $25 million. The next year's amount grew to $30 million, and the projected amount for this grant offering for 2005–2006 is $50 million. The best thing about this opportunity is that some of the overall amount has been reserved for "minigrants," distributions of $50,000 or less. This enables smaller organizations that do good work to break into the government funding system without having to prove that they can manage a multimillion-dollar budget. The CCF minigrants are the best way for grassroots organizations with strong community partners to initiate a government grant segment of their overall development plan. Keep in mind, however, that this is an extremely competitive process and that the application process and procedures for a $50,000 grant are often, but not always, as draining as for a $5 million grant. Details can be found at www.fbci.gov or on the HHS Web site, www.hhs.gov. Search on "Compassion Capital Fund grants."

Government Dollars at the State Level

Fully 80 to 90 percent of all social and welfare dollars is sent back to the states in the form of block grants. These large sums of money are then left to the states' social services departments to divvy up according to their particular needs and fancy. Sometimes, but not always, the state agency will issue requests for proposals (RFPs) or requests for application (RFAs), or some other similar announcement, notifying the general public and people who deliver services that there are grant or contract opportunities available from the state for which they may submit a proposal for a contract or grant.

What happens to the other 10 to 20 percent of the collected funds received by federal agencies? Those dollars become "discretionary funds," which are used for projects and programs at the discretion of the federal agency staff. Sometimes projects are funded out of these discretionary federal budgets at the state and county levels. But generally, if you are seeking a government grant, you are better off going to your state or county agencies for support. They have more to give out, they understand the needs of the region, and theoretically at least, they keep a closer eye on the outcomes and results.

Unfortunately, this practice is not as streamlined as it was originally designed to be. Some states don't comply with federal regulations that require state agencies to keep funds separate and not commingle dollars. The best example of this problem is demonstrated in the response some states are giving regarding the Faith-Based and Community Initiative. A large percentage of the federal dollars sent back to states have the Charitable Choice laws attached to them. Charitable Choice requires that state and federal agencies not discriminate against faith-based organizations in their contracting practices. However, when the money reaches the state, it is often deposited into the state's general budget without respect for the federal regulations.

So some states feel justified in holding a policy of "not spending government money on religious activities" or "not issuing state revenue to an inherently religious organization." These states often have a so-called Blaine amendment that they use to "protect the public trust" with respect to how state government uses tax funds. The problem with these arguments is that these states are conveniently ignoring the federal laws implementing Charitable Choice and prohibiting the commingling of funds. It is as if they forgot that the bulk of their social service dollars came from the federal system in the first place. Exhibit 6.5 provides some help if you encounter the need to address this issue.

Exhibit 6.5
What to Do If Officials Ignore Charitable Choice

Charitable Choice has been the law of the land for certain federal funds since it was first adopted as part of the federal welfare reform law (PRWORA) by Congress and the President in August, 1996. It covers federal funds for welfare and Welfare-to-Work services, Community Action Agencies, and certain drug treatment programs. Charitable Choice is a federal requirement that state and local governments cannot avoid when they accept those funds.

However, for Charitable Choice to make a difference for a faith-based group that wishes to collaborate with government programs, state and local authorities first have to put the new rules into effect. They must ensure that their own procurement regulations and practices have been made to comply with Charitable Choice.

Exhibit 6.5
What to Do If Officials Ignore Charitable Choice, Cont'd.

Instead, many state and local governments have yet to come into compliance with Charitable Choice. In too many cases, officials do not even know that Charitable Choice has established new rules for procurement. In other cases, officials have chosen not to comply with Charitable Choice, arguing that the rules conflict with the constitution (federal or state) or with state or local laws forbidding religious discrimination. Or they assert that compliance is useless because faith-based organizations are not large enough or mature enough to contract with government. In some places officials refuse to comply because they are beholden to existing relationships with nonprofit organizations.

Faith-based organizations should not be surprised if they encounter blank stares or opposition when they approach public officials to claim their right under Charitable Choice to compete to provide services.

But don't give up! Instead, be a change agent! Prayerfully play a part in helping to open up the public square to full participation by religious service organizations. Start by informing yourself fully about Charitable Choice: how it protects faith-based organizations, what limits it places on religious activities, and how it protects people who need services.

Educate

If you get the brush-off when you ask how your faith-based organization can compete to provide services the government seeks to buy . . .

- If the officials just don't know, share with them the *Guide to Charitable Choice* or "Charitable Choice 101: An Introduction."
- If the local officials are resistant, go higher up: find out who in the welfare or workforce development system is in charge of community outreach or relations with community or religious groups. This person may know about Charitable Choice, may be looking exactly for opportunities to link with faith communities, and may be able to help overcome the local resistance.

Challenge

Local resistance may reflect indifference or opposition to Charitable Choice by the entire welfare or workforce development agency, the attorney general, the legislature, or the governor . . .

- If so, you may want to make implementation of Charitable Choice a key priority on behalf of your organization, other faith-based providers, and the poor, who deserve the best assistance they can get. Join with others, if you can, and search for a sympathetic legislator, or someone in the governor's office who knows the power of God's love unleashed in service, or an official in the welfare system who understands that faith is the root of love, not a toxin to be kept hidden away. Start to educate the officials and win their support for expanded collaboration that respects the special character of faith-based organizations.
- If you are prevented from competing to provide services or, after being selected as a provider, discover that the conditions of the contract violate Charitable Choice, consult a knowledgeable lawyer to see what your recourse is. A word from the lawyer may be enough to help the officials recall what the law actually requires. Or you may have to decide whether to challenge the violation in court, generate publicity about the violation, or organize public pressure.

Work Around

If officials resist putting Charitable Choice into practice, you may wish to try alternatives (perhaps while also pressing for compliance):

- Build strong relations with local officials so that they can see how your programs would assist their clients. Their desire to collaborate may outweigh their resistance to Charitable Choice.
- Remind officials about the great challenge posed by the families remaining on welfare, the significant surpluses they have in their welfare accounts, and the broad scope the federal government has given them to try innovative approaches to assisting needy families. Propose that they work "outside the box" with you and with other faith-based ministries, emphasizing the importance of new approaches and the growing public consensus in favor of government collaboration with faith communities.

Exhibit 6.5
What to Do If Officials Ignore Charitable Choice, Cont'd.

- If officials claim that they cannot contract with your organization because it is too religious or inexperienced, see if you can subcontract with some group that the government has accepted as a provider. Whether religious, secular, or for-profit, that group may be looking exactly for an organization like yours that is rooted in the community and may find your faith basis to be an asset, not a liability.
- Your ministry might join with other ministries or congregations in a faith-based consortium that partners with an experienced religious contractor. Officials are familiar with groups such as the Salvation Army, Catholic Charities, and Lutheran Social Services, and many of these groups are used to dealing with government requirements. They may be willing to be the contract administrator and intermediary between the faith-based consortium and skeptical government officials.
- If officials insist that faith-based groups must be excluded from government money or you prayerfully determine that the government's conditions are unacceptable, you may want to explore the possibilities of a nonfinancial relationship with the public programs. Officials may be willing to refer clients to you on an occasional basis. And they even may be happy to enter into a formal referral arrangement, convinced that you can offer their clients essential assistance, despite their (false) belief that government money must not flow to you.

Legal Resources

A Guide to Charitable Choice: The Rules of Section 104 of the 1996 Federal Welfare Law Governing State Cooperation with Faith-Based Social-Service Providers (Center for Public Justice and Center for Law and Religious Freedom, 1997); (410) 571-6300 or www.cpjustice.org.

Gammon and Grange (www.gandglaw.com), (703) 761-5000. Ask for Peter Rathbun, Rick Campanelli, or Chip Grange. Will refer to local counsel if appropriate.

Alliance Defense Fund (www.alliancedefensefund.org), (602) 953-1200. Ask to be referred to a staff attorney or to local counsel.

Christian Legal Society, (703) 642-1070. Explain your concern and ask to be directed to a staff attorney or to one of the hundreds of CLS member attorneys throughout the country.

Source: Used by permission of Stanley W. Carlson-Thies and the Center for Public Justice.

Fortunately, HHS passed the new Equal Treatment Regulations on August 16, 2004. Some important inclusions of these regulations, according to Stanley Carlson-Thies are the following:

- Funding decision makers cannot discriminate for or against a provider because of the provider's religious character or affiliation.
- No faith-based provider may be excluded as being "too religious" or "sectarian."
- Providers may retain their religious name, mission statement, and board members even if based on religious affiliation.
- Providers may offer inherently religious activities separately from grant and contract funded services.
- FBOs do retain their federal exemption to hire on a religious basis unless the state program statute forbids it.
- FBOs may appeal to the Religious Freedom Restoration Act against state restrictions on religious staffing.
- FBOs are subject to state and local procurement law restrictions on religious staffing but can appeal to their rights under the equal treatment regulations and the First Amendment.

These new regulations apply to all HHS discretionary, formula, and block grant funds, all other state and local funds that are commingled with federal funds within financial relations such as contracts, grants, subcontracts, subgrants, vouchers, certificates, and indirect or beneficiary choice contracting.

Although these new regulations clear up many questions regarding faith-based–government partnerships, it will take a while for many states to observe and implement the changes.

Another way states avoid contracting with faith-based organizations (including churches) is to keep contract opportunities a secret. Most states have a preferred list of service providers they have worked with for years, and inviting new prospective partners to the process can simply be too much trouble to deal with. By keeping grant opportunities secret, the state agencies retain the control they are comfortable having. If they do need a new contractor, they often assume the attitude, "Don't call us; we'll call you!" They have their special select groups they call on when the need arises. This is somewhat understandable since the process of state contracting is so complicated and fraught with the potential for mishandling of funds or legal action. State and county directors need some assurance that their contractors will not present a liability. When an organization proves reliable, its integrity is rewarded with new or extended contracts. Thus current contractors have a huge advantage over newcomers to the game.

My state gives the impression that it welcomes new proposals for service, but this may be for appearances only. There is no departmental guideline that instructs the agency to read new proposals even if they do arrive in the mail. The common practice of ignoring new applicants obviously makes it difficult for new contenders to acquire a grant or contract. So be wise; do your homework. Be prepared to put in the time to ask lots of questions. Record the names and responses you are given when you call. The answers you get can change, depending on to whom you speak. You'll appear more savvy if you can refer to a previous conversation you had with Ms. Jones last Tuesday that doesn't match what you are being told the fourth time around. Perusing new grant proposals and adding another site visit to the case worker's calendar is truly rocking the proverbial boat in many cases. You need to give this person compelling reasons to include you in the contract pool.

OK, you're ready to begin the process of applying for a government grant. Let's walk through the process and stop just shy of actually filling out the forms. I can't teach grantwriting in this volume, and there are many great courses available that are listed on our Web site. Keep in mind that grantwriting is a profession; it should not be entered into lightly. But let's walk as far as we can up the path so you can get a better idea of just what to expect in pursuing a government grant.

Preliminary Steps to Preparing a Government Grant

You should be glad to know that state and county grants are usually less demanding than federal grants in terms of preparation. In my state of Washington, some counties offer a "countywide application process," so if you are seeking a government contract or partnership in one city, you may submit the same proposal for another city within the same county. It is called the "common application." Check this out in your state and county.

Also, a county grant will not require quite so much in the way of background information on your organization. I guess the authorities figure that since you are already operating in the county, they probably know a little about you already. This cuts down on your preparation time and aggravation. However, county contracts are not as large as federal and state contracts, and normally you must reapply each year for the same contract, whereas federal grants are usually for eighteen months to five years in duration.

Following are some steps to take to prepare a government grant.

1. Research appropriate opportunities by going to federal and state Web sites. If you don't know where to find those sites, go to your state's general Web site (for example, www.montana.gov) and follow any leads you find there. Usually there will be links to your social service arm of government or to the state agencies that contract with private and nonprofit businesses. In my state, the Office of Financial Management has been a great source of information. Your state probably has something similar with very current data.

   For federal opportunities, go to www.firstgov.gov or www.fbci.gov or to the individual departments that handle your area of service, such as the Department of Labor at www.dol.gov. Many more links are listed on our Web site, www.josseybass.com/go/esau. Keep in mind that each year, all government agencies, from federal to local, reissue their contract opportunities (RFPs and RFAs). Some are for twelve months and some are for as long as five years. Early spring is when most of the new opportunities are announced. But looking at previous years' offerings will give you a good idea of what will be announced in the coming year. Just poke around and print out the lists that match your work.

2. Highlight the listings that you want to pursue and pass them around to your teammates. Get feedback and advice from your helpers because you won't want to tackle this project alone. Consider the deadline date! For your first few grant proposals, you should allow about a month to prepare each. The time factor should influence your decision greatly. Decide who is willing to do which parts—for example, one person should prepare the financial portion, another should design the program part to match the description of the grant, and a third could commit to doing the final writing. Pay special attention to any

required matching funds. Don't pursue a grant that lists a required match of 50 percent if you don't have that amount standing by or committed from a partner. Today, matching funds may sometimes also take the form of in-kind goods and services. Just be sure to check out that detail before investing too much time in a particular grant proposal. Talk it over and get an idea of how much time and effort the project will truly take.

3. Call or e-mail the contact person listed on the RFP (grant announcement). Have a list of questions written out so that you can get the most out of this conversation. Describe in fine detail what you do and how you are planning to approach this grant opportunity; then ask for the manager's opinion. Take good notes. They may tell you things that are not included in the RFP but are essential elements nonetheless.

4. Do more research. See who obtained the previous awards; this information is usually posted on the federal Web sites. If it is a state grant you are pursuing, ask the contact person where you can find the previous award information. Read up on all the available history of the grant, and learn what made those applications attractive. Pay close attention to the details, such as location of service, population served, numbers served, and what made that proposal unique. If possible, talk to the previous grantee to find out what worked and what didn't. Also, get the range of funding for this particular grant. Don't ask for $100,000 if last year's amount was in the $20,000-to-$30,000 range.

5. Pick apart the pieces of the RFP. Read it several times; become so familiar with it that you know exactly what it is asking for. RFPs usually have a long list of seemingly arbitrary requirements—but they're definitely not arbitrary! If the RFP wants you to incorporate several community partners, don't list only two. Go out and recruit four or five different organizations, ranging from secular nonprofits to private businesses to public schools and so on, if that's what the RFP requires.

6. Create a timeline to organize your work. Be realistic, not idealistic. Consider how many people are working on the grant. Do they all have other obligations, or do they have unlimited time to invest in the process? Allow extra time for review and revisions. Your timeline might look something like the one in Figure 6.1.

Figure 6.1
A Grant Proposal Timeline

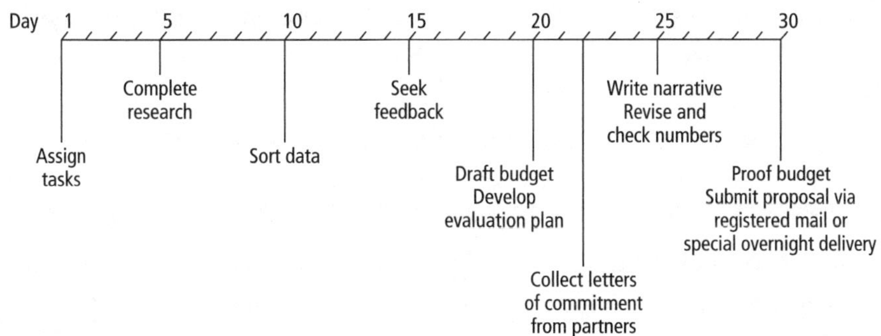

7. Hold a focus group to discuss the possibility of working with your potential partners. Incorporating findings from a focus group tells the readers that you did diligent research before applying for a major grant. Include some of the comments made at this meeting in your narrative section to prove that you have thought things through thoroughly. That's worth several points in your final grant score.

8. Get to work! Or hire a grantwriter. . . .

County- or Community-Level Contracting

Most states funnel dollars down to the counties to meet social needs. Counties often have a substantial funding for juvenile justice, substance abuse treatment and rehabilitation, after-school child care, food- and job-related services to the homeless, and health concerns. They also administer most of the homeless and temporary shelter contracts. Usually, these opportunities are not quite so demanding in terms of proposal preparation. They also tend to be more realistic dollar amounts for start-up or younger organizations that are new to government partnership.

Be forewarned that it is tempting to shoot for the moon and apply for a half-million-dollar federal grant. But unless you can demonstrate that you have managed that sum of money, ideally even more, over an extended period of time, it is absolutely out of the question that you would be considered for such an award.

A more realistic award for a first-time applicant might be $10,000 to $20,000 through a subcontract award. If you remain flexible and open to working with others as a part of a system, you're more likely to get a foot in the door to county contracting. Once you have proved that your staff and volunteers are reliable and energetic, your reputation will gain a higher profile in circles that will open up future opportunities.

For information on county funding opportunities, call your General Services Division or similar office at the county seat and ask where to find contract listings. Begin small and work hard to grow your operations. The value of this approach is twofold: you give yourself the needed time to learn the ropes in the practical sense, and you set yourself up for a state or federal grant down the road. The larger entities will take you more seriously if you have jogged around the local block before climbing Mount Everest.

A good way to market your services to your county government centers is to establish a relationship with your county board of supervisors or equivalent elected body. We'll talk more about this approach in Chapter Eight, but remember that in our business, as in most businesses, it's who you know that opens doors. Identify a champion or two to herald your cause. Give your boosters enough good information to boast about, and you might end up with a contract just by filling out some standard forms.

Site Visits

Most first-time government award recipients get a site visit from the regional agency that oversees each particular grant. For example, if you run a teen shelter and you've applied for a juvenile justice grant to conduct intensive counseling sessions for your constituents, the state or regional justice official will probably want to walk through your facility and observe how things operate on a normal day.

You may want to ask this official in advance of the visit what specific things he or she is looking for. Will health code compliance or emergency procedures be inspected? Will client files be examined and checked for documentation of progress or regression? The official may not tell you precisely what he or she is looking for, but it doesn't hurt to ask. Then (here's where it helps to know others who do similar work in your field) call another shelter and ask if it has had a site visit from the state. It never hurts to do your homework and be prepared for a site visit. And in fact, a site visit could make or break your chances for landing a grant.

Getting the Grant

David Mills, a good friend and expert grants manager for We Care America, tells of the two scariest days in the life of a grantwriter: the second is the day you receive notification you were not awarded; the first is the day you get the grant—because now you are obliged to perform all the work you said you would do in your proposal!

Even a small grant (anything under $50,000) has specific expectations attached from day one of your funding cycle. Make sure you familiarize yourself and your staff thoroughly from day one so that you don't jeopardize any portion of your work. Remember, noncompliance is grounds for canceling a grant contract. Make special calendar entries for each report that is due, and prepare those reports in plenty of time to submit them correctly.

Receiving a government grant is truly an impressive accomplishment. It validates your work in the eyes of your colleagues and community partners. It gives your work momentum and the boost needed to function at the "next level." It attracts attention from other funding agencies within and beyond government circles. It also allows you to breathe a sigh of relief, knowing that you have solid funding support for the next few months.

Don't wait too long to begin the application process for the next grant you will need when the current grant expires. Whether you were awarded for one year or three, you'll want to stay diversified in your development plan. Don't regard your first public sector grant as the answer to all your funding needs. Keep researching other government and private opportunities. Now that you have secured a public grant, you will have a greater chance at landing another, as long as you manage your operations carefully.

The time seems to fly by, and you need to be lining up the funds to sustain the program your grant allowed you to initiate. Most government funding is directed to new or innovative approaches to social conditions. Rarely does a government agency want to fund work you have been doing for several years using your faithful donor's dollars. A typical government grant will be awarded to a project that represents a unique partnership, takes a unique approach to solving an old problem, or targets a demographic group that isn't being served by other programs in the area.

When you land a government grant for these types of projects, you need to regard that grant as "seed money" because that is often how the government views it. Grantors want you to assure them that you will be able to sustain this new project long after the government dollars are used up. This is why community-level partnerships are such an asset to a proposal. The funder views a broad-based partnership as a better bet for sustaining the project beyond the life of the grant. Diverse funding sources and community relationships insure against the demise of a good program when one resource dries up.

After reading about government partnerships and the grant process, you may decide that it is not for you. This is OK; in fact, it's very common. You may, however, decide that some parts of this process might work for you, and you will investigate further. Each organization is different; each leadership team has its own personality and strengths. You may tailor the partnership process to fit your organizational culture and seek grants that match your specific area of service without giving up too much.

Remain flexible, learn from others, do your homework, and think creatively. You could double your effectiveness and reach by jumping into the government partnership boat. Just do so with caution and good advice. Become well acquainted with Stanley Carlson-Thies's work in this chapter and in Resource C.

Once you have some experience dealing with government agencies and their representatives, you will be prepared to leverage that experience in advocacy and lobbying efforts on behalf of your constituents. The next chapter provides specific guidelines for interacting in a meaningful way with public and elected officials.

chapter
SEVEN

Considering Advocacy

When, Why, and How Should You Advocate in the Public Sector?

I believe that advocating on behalf of the folks you serve is a responsibility. But is it also a privilege and a right. The challenge is figuring out how to do it, what is allowed by law, where to go for information, and how much of your precious resources to designate for advocacy efforts. All these matters will be addressed in this chapter, again on an introductory level. I'll show you how to design your own organizational advocacy plan to use however you prefer.

Chapter Two explained the importance of knowing your mission, vision, and values statements so well that you can recite them at any time, anywhere, to anyone. Advocacy takes that principle one step further and becomes deliberate about sharing your information to affect public policy. *Advocacy* is the process of representing an interest or concern in the public arena. It is closely aligned with, but not identical to *lobbying,* which is defined as an attempt to influence specific legislation. Because faith-based social service is an emerging policy trend, it is essential that you present your ideas, accomplishments, and future plans in terms that policymakers understand and want to support. By effectively communicating with policymakers and high-profile public figures, each organization or leader plays a part in the national effort of expanding faith-based service delivery.

Just as the Sierra Club has led the charge in the environmental movement for the past twenty-five years and Planned Parenthood has defended the right to choose abortion, faith-based service providers can be very effective in promoting and expanding widespread contracts and partnerships at the grassroots level. The secret to the success of most social movements rests with truly committed people at the community level. "There is nothing so strong as the heart of a volunteer" is a statement that has been proved over and over throughout history. We must not expect progress on this issue to come from the federal government alone. We have a responsibility to create the groundswell of interest and action at the local and state levels if we want to see real advances in faith-based social contracts.

But how do we do this? How do we make our voice heard? How do we handle the opposition, which is undeniably out there? What about the state governments that refuse to observe the federal mandates affecting our work? Whom will we find to "champion" our cause other than a few folks at the White House or in Congress? What are the intermediate levels on which we could be working? Should we dedicate time to advocacy at the expense of direct service? How much will it cost to advocate effectively? If strength is found in numbers, whom do we link up with to make a "bigger splash"? Read on for specific help.

THE ADVANTAGES OF ADVOCACY

Advocacy is a combination of marketing, teaching, and vision-casting. It should be a creative approach to shoring up interest and support for your organizational values and mission. But beware of concentrating so hard on your organization that you neglect your clients. Never lose your "line of sight" to your clients; doing so will cause mission drift. The most effective advocacy work puts the clients' needs and conditions out front. So your best approach will be sensitive to your clients and based on facts. Successful advocacy can bring unlimited advantages to your organization, including the following:

- Name recognition in the community
- Broad-based financial support
- Friends in key places of influence
- Increased volunteer support
- Respect from political authorities
- Inclusion in related discussions and decision-making sessions
- Partnership opportunities

- Leadership opportunities
- Media attention
- Advanced news of political, social, or financial developments

Choosing an issue on which to focus your advocacy efforts can be tricky. *An issue is a potential solution to a problem.* While there may be obvious and urgent concerns that affect your ministry, such as funding cuts in your state budget, it may not be the most important thing for you to address during the current legislative session or county council hearing. You and your team may need to step back and analyze other concerns that could have farther-reaching effects on your area of service. For example, your state agency may be considering a new policy that would force your organization to terminate your current mentors due to past criminal records. So even though funding issues are important, policy issues can render your program obsolete!

A good way to analyze your situation is to use an advocacy checklist, such as the one presented in Exhibit 7.1.

Once you have selected your issue or set of issues to address in your advocacy efforts, you'll want to balance your approach fairly evenly between offensive and defensive activities.

Offensive advocacy consists of defining problems and issues in ways that your organization can address and solve. It involves taking charge of the issues and shaping them to your advantage. If your community has a homeless problem and you operate a shelter, you will be considered an expert in the matter and should offer your opinion on ways to address it. You might advocate on behalf of the homeless population by writing articles for the local newspaper. You could explain to the uninformed population that 75 to 80 percent of homelessness may be traced to substance abuse and unstable mental health; therefore, shelters such as yours should receive state funding to beef up programs and counseling for substance abuse.

Or in the case of the juvenile truancy problem, you may want to advocate on behalf of retaining screened and trained mentors who have a minor criminal record due to the fact that they understand the system and can convince kids to stay away from the influences that could lead them to incarceration. You will be respected for your position because your program has had success with such mentors.

Exhibit 7.1
Advocacy Checklist for Choosing Issues

1. Does this issue affect our agency mission?

   How—negatively? Positively? Give examples.

2. Would promoting this issue detract from our agency mission?

   In what ways? Financially, structurally, cost of time and staff?

   Would the agency suffer if we embark on this cause? How?

3. Do our stakeholders have an emotional attachment to this issue?

   Who would join in our efforts and support the cause?

   Will we encounter resistance? From whom?

4. Do the advantages outweigh the disadvantages regardless of the outcome?

   Will the result be worth the investment even if we don't prevail?

5. How shall we define success?

   By what measures and terms?

   In what amount of time and cost?

   What is the probability of success?

6. Do we have resources to commit to this cause now?

   If not now, will we in the future?

   Who will determine this?

   What will be the extent of those resources?

7. Can we remain stable during a time of change or transition?

   Are board and staff structures strong and resilient?

   Can we endure the loss or gain of constituents?

   Is there a mechanism for withdrawing if that should prove necessary?

Offensive action would also include serving on committees or community task forces that address your issues. By inserting your organization into the decision-making or problem-solving process, you position yourself as an advocate. This is a particularly advantageous form of advocacy because you become part of a select, high-profile group with public recognition. You also reap the benefit of learning from other, more experienced professionals in your area of expertise.

Defensive advocacy is more controversial. This method involves taking a stand when it may not be popular. It could mean challenging a popular view or person, which will invite criticism and consequences for a broader movement of which you are only a small part. For example, the right-to-life folks challenge abortion laws on every front and at every level. They do important defensive advocacy by continually drawing the public's attention to the social, physical, and emotional dangers of abortion. About half the American population agrees with the right-to-life position, but their primary message is a negative one: overturn *Roe* v. *Wade* or at least impose tighter restrictions on the availability of abortion. They are defending the "rights of the unborn" by trying to convince key decision makers to *undo* something rather than to *do* something.

Effective defensive advocacy is harder to define than effective offensive advocacy. Sometimes effective defensive advocacy may be defined by negative press coverage. The rationale is "at least our name was mentioned in the evening news coverage, and people who care about our issue now know that we exist." Defending your position on policy issues is just as important as promoting your cause. However, in order to defend your position, you must understand what the opposition is saying. This is a form of taking stock or evaluating the landscape.

There is no better way to appear authoritative about your issue than by analyzing the situation from both sides. Often a good way to begin a public comment on an issue is by stating the arguments right up front:

> "They say kids are going to have sex anyway. . . ."
>
> "Some people believe that all drug addicts share their needles. . . ."
>
> "The governor thinks our education system works just fine. . . ."

A true advocate is never caught off-guard or unsure of what opponents think. Doing some homework will pay off. This type of opening remark will get attention quickly and cause people to listen even if they disagree with you.

THE RESPONSIBILITIES OF ADVOCACY

Once you have created your marketing tools, such as a brochure, a Web site, or a newsletter, you will want to put these before as many strategic parties as possible. Elected officials, your government social service agency heads and contract directors, state legislators, and governors' policy advisers should all be at the top of your advocacy list to receive your promotional tools. Making sure of this will take research and lots of phone calls and e-mail. This is a great job for a volunteer.

It is your responsibility to help your coworkers understand that in order for your beliefs and ideas to gain acceptance and support, concerted public relations and advocacy work must be done. In the case of faith-based issues, everything is new and uncertain. This should be viewed as an exciting opportunity. You and your supporters can play a big role in shaping the local attitude toward faith-based social services. Don't let the void and lack of definition slip into negative territory. Seize the day and become the defining force for your cause! But as with all controversial issues, more is accomplished by proceeding with respect and firm yet gentle dialogue.

DEVELOPING AN ADVOCACY PLAN

Creating your organizational advocacy plan sounds complicated but doesn't have to be. In fact, you may take each of the steps listed here and begin today. As with many project plans, the key to making progress is to just jump in somewhere and allow the system to take shape as you work. Give yourself or your volunteer enough leeway to stumble and restart. For example, you miss an opportunity to meet the mayor at a community rally, you forget to ask your board members for introductions at a party, you miss a legislative hearing on your issue, your editorial in the newspaper is misinterpreted, you fail to provide your legislator with information he or she requested—you get the idea.

Luckily, most people are very forgiving and have a short memory of such things. By implementing the following five simple steps, you will develop an effective advocacy plan that will produce fruit.

Five-Step Advocacy Plan

1. Identify the key regional and state influencers of your issue.
2. Establish a friendly working relationship with each of them.

   Teach them what you want them to know.

   Provide resource material and updates on the issue.

Volunteer to provide expert testimony when needed.

Bring others to public hearings and related events.

3. Ask a few of them to champion your cause.

Invite them to speak at gatherings.

Do their homework for them, and feed them supportive data.

Refer to them publicly as your "advocate."

Tell them about events they should attend and why.

4. Educate constituents about your issues and ask for their public support.

Provide fact sheets and sound bites.

Solicit constituents' ideas and help in getting the word out.

5. Begin a media campaign.

Use helpers to submit editorials to local media.

Contact local radio hosts and offer an interview on the issue.

Host an event and invite TV news crews to come film it.

These tasks can be completed in a week's time with help. Once the ball is rolling in this direction, many more introductions and opportunities will automatically follow.

The most difficult part of advocacy is keeping current with your information and supportive contacts. That underscores the need for reliable help. I suggest finding one person to oversee your advocacy plan, and explaining that you expect that person to build a team for each media type, government contact, and constituent training. Your advocacy team leader should be responsible for keeping up with news and policy that affect your organization. This frees staff to concentrate on direct service, fundraising, board relations, and all the other demands of running a grassroots nonprofit. The action chart presented in Exhibit 7.2 should provide some guidance in advocacy planning.

Here are some hints to help you identify strategic contacts:

1. Call the League of Women Voters and ask who all of your elected officials are. You will need to give your address to determine your legislative and congressional districts if you don't know them. Write down all the names and contact information they can give you, including the names of legislative aides (LAs).

Exhibit 7.2
Public Policy Action Chart

Deadline	Action	Responsible Party	Budget	Desired Outcome
Jan. 31, 2006	Complete IRS election filing	Manager	Public policy budget raised	Freedom to lobby within guidelines
	Perform SWOT analysis for initiating advocacy	Board, staff, volunteers	Public policy budget	A clear understanding of what is involved
	Complete one session board training of Charitable Choice	Manager	Public policy budget raised	Informed and equipped board members
	Continue the quest for state decision makers re Charitable Choice	Entire board, staff, volunteers	Public policy budget raised	Greater acceptance of FBOs by government officials
Feb. 28, 2006	Minimum five meetings with public officials	Board and staff	Public policy budget	Support and promote Charitable Choice in our state
	Publish fact sheet and circulate to partner organizations	Manager	Public policy budget	Inform other FBOs Recruit support
	Initiate state FBO coalition and Web site	Board, staff, volunteers	—	Gain strength in numbers

Mar. 31, 2006	Minimum five meetings with public officials	Board, staff, volunteers, coalition members	Public policy budget	Support and promote Charitable Choice in our state
	Organize, advertise event with Dr. Johnson in April	Staff with volunteers	Special fund ($10,000 needed)	Four to five thousand attending; wider acceptance and promotion of Charitable Choice
	Continue to build coalition	All	Public policy budget	Added strength, added influence
	Assess progress to date	All	Public policy budget	Decide how to proceed
Apr. 30, 2006	Concentrate on lecture event; hold event	All	Special fund	Great response to information delivered; changed attitudes; acceptance of Charitable Choice
	Five more meetings with officials	All	Public policy budget	Improved relationships; favorable support
	Follow up on lecture	Staff	Public policy budget	Feedback from public, constituents, government; begin to see more contracts to FBOs

Exhibit 7.2
Public Policy Action Chart, Cont'd.

Deadline	Action	Responsible Party	Budget	Desired Outcome
May 31, 2006	Joint coalition meeting	All	Public policy budget	Make decisions on what to do next
	Follow up with public officials	Staff, board	Public policy budget	Solicit support, approve Charitable Choice state mandates; recommend FBO contract
	Publish fact sheet, circulate through member organizations	Manager	Public policy budget	Greater understanding of our issues
	Form unlikely alliance of state legislators	Board	Public policy budget	Draw attention of full legislature and media; more FBO contracts
June 30, 2006	Request that legislature formally adopt Charitable Choice as passed by Congress	Coalition	Public policy budget	Formal legislation adopted in our state, more government contracts for FBOs
	Continue to develop new relationships with public officials	Coalition	Individual agencies	End to the battle for the "level playing field"

LAs can often be your greatest source of information and support. Develop relationships with everyone in these offices so that you know them on a first-name basis and, even more important, so that they know who you are when you call and what kind of work you do.

2. Ask the legislator, county council member, or government agency official for names of individuals who have jurisdiction over the areas of policy that your work affects. If you want to establish a neighborhood day care that would contract with government, you need to figure out who is in decision-making positions at the local, county, and state levels. All state governments operate on the national model of committees with chairs who decide which bills will be heard and voted on. You need to be informed on the issues each committee is discussing during the legislative or council session. Always be respectful in your use of the correct personal titles. Refer to legislators as "Senator X" or "Representative Y." Use their first name only if *they* suggest it.

3. Attend some of the community meetings that relate to your work, such as city council meetings, community action groups, school board meetings, and national support groups such as the American Heart Association, Special Olympics, and the Fatherhood Forum. While there, ask lots of questions! Make it your business to find out all you can about who attends and leads the group. On what areas do these people focus? What are their objectives? How might your organization assist or gain from becoming associated with this group?

Simply delivering the goods to the appropriate office is not enough. These expensive materials will be dropped into a file or a drawer, never to be seen again, if you don't take the time to use them properly. You must teach your audience about the importance of your work. This requires developing that ever-important personal relationship.

Once you have determined who makes decisions and influences others, you have a potential champion. Ask for an appointment in the next week to discuss an issue that affects your organization or area of service. Have a critical reason for the requested meeting. Estimate how long the appointment will last (twenty minutes is about the maximum you will be given). Use compelling reasons when requesting a meeting: for example, "I would like to come see the senator for about twenty minutes to discuss "how recent budget cuts are going to drastically affect our services," "how our organization can alleviate some of the logjam in the juvenile justice system," "how our summer school for low-income youth could triple its enrollment with the senator's help," or "what to do about the fact that the warehouse we use for our food distribution program is being rezoned and we're being tossed out."

Preparing for Your Meeting

Before your meeting day, help yourself by doing a little homework. Ask an enthusiastic volunteer or a politically interested student to research your potential champion. Give your helper the staff contact information and suggest that he or she search the Internet for any and all information about your "special person." Find out the person's opinions, how he or she voted on related issues, and what he or she has written on the topic. Of course, you'll want to know if this leader has a particular faith heritage. Does he or she attend church? Might you have a common interest, such as youth sports? Thanks to this research, when you meet, you are armed with facts that you can mention or challenge. Your host will be impressed that you took the time to prepare and not waste your valuable minutes together. He will be more likely to invite you back, respond to your next call, or refer to your organization in a public interview.

Ask how many people you may bring with you to your meeting. Keep it to individuals who can answer specific questions and lend credibility to your cause. Avoid bringing people who only want to "shake the mayor's hand" or take a photograph. The mayor will accommodate you but will probably not take you as seriously as you'd like. A group of two or three experts is probably best for such a meeting.

Your Initial Meeting

First impressions count. As you enter your public official's office, maintain the utmost respect for the staff as well as the official. Staff have a huge influence on elected people, who juggle five times more detail each day than they can truly manage. They rely on staff for things like first impressions. Refer to the elected by title and last name unless you have been invited to use the person's first name.

Arrive no more than five minutes early. Most public officials' offices are too small to accommodate lots of waiting people. Never be even one second late. Your host may be late, and often is, but you have no such luxury. Always call ahead to the staff if you are held up in traffic or otherwise delayed. This conveys respect for everyone's time and a command of the situation, even though things seem out of your control.

Once into your appointment, monitor your time carefully. Remember that a great many people request this person's attention every day. Respect his or her time and understand the potential for distraction. Whether you're talking to a city councilman or the governor, expect to have no more than twenty minutes of undivided attention. Make those minutes count! Have documents prepared to hand over; then boil the information down to "Here's what we are asking of you. . . ." If you can't supply the answer to that question, postpone your interview until you know exactly what you want the person to do for you, your organization, or your cause.

Let one voice be the spokesperson for your contingent. Rehearse the conversation prior to the meeting so that your time will be as productive as possible. Be as direct as possible, for example: "Mayor Johnson, on behalf of the three thousand homeless folks on the streets of our city every night, we are asking you to recommend our Safe and Sound Shelter as a contractor for city services for a two-year period. Here's why. . . ." If the mayor professes to have no control over the situation, ask if you can refer to him or her as a supporter of your organization as you seek to gain a contract through other channels.

Remember that public officials will probably not seek out your organization without some personal contact from your leadership. If you are waiting for the local welfare office to come knocking on your door asking if it might refer clients to your shelter, you will wait forever. Don't expect the decision makers to come to you. Jump in and become a player! Educate and inform the official using Exhibit 7.3.

A Personal Story

For two consecutive years, a state legislator in my state drafted and acted as the prime sponsor of a bill that would require our state social service agency to provide an information service to faith-based and community groups. The bill had no money attached to it, so it should have passed easily into state law. It didn't. For various reasons too complicated to explain here, the bill failed to come to a full vote of the legislature and died after the second session attempt.

Exhibit 7.3
Charitable Choice: Top Ten Tips for Public Officials

1. Inform Recipients. When a provider is faith-based, make sure recipients know about its religious character, their freedom not to engage in religious activities, and their right to receive services from an alternative provider.
2. Alternatives. Be prepared to offer an accessible, high-quality alternative service to any recipient who objects to a faith-based provider. Make advance arrangements with a different provider in the same location, plan access and transportation to a nearby provider, or maintain a residual government capacity to provide services.
3. Religion Is Not Toxic. Ensure the religious liberty of recipients without presuming that faith is toxic. A recipient troubled by a faith-based provider may want another religious provider, not a secular service. Many of the needy are people of faith and desire assistance that acknowledges their convictions.
4. Allies. Collaboration means working together to achieve the common aim of assisting the needy while also respecting the differences between government and faith-based organizations. Allied providers are more than vendors; they retain their freedom, their right to advocate on behalf of clients, and their responsibility to speak to policy.
5. Employment Rights. The biggest barrier to greater cooperation between the faith community and public welfare is not allowing faith-based providers to hire and fire on the basis of religion. Some religious organizations choose to hire without regard to faith, but many insist on religious criteria in order to retain their distinctive missions. Contract language forbidding them to use religion in hiring is illegal under Charitable Choice and must be eliminated.

6. Vouchers. Voucher arrangements are better than contracting for preserving the independence of faith-based organizations and giving recipients choice. Where possible, redesign services and procurement policies so that a range of organizations can provide services and each recipient has the chance to select the most effective and compatible provider.
7. Structures for Cooperation. Many congregations and faith-based nonprofits are too small to handle the service volume of a typical contract. To utilize their strengths and allow them to participate, alternatives are needed: voucherized services, contracting with a nonprofit intermediary that links congregations, a lead agency that subcontracts with smaller groups.
8. Training and Assistance. Government can help prepare faith-based organizations to provide authorized services by offering training in contracting, record-keeping, and regulations and by assisting them in planning and presenting service proposals. Such assistance should be offered to all small-scale nonprofits and community organizations.
9. Affirmative Outreach. Many faith-based organizations have not been part of the human services system. They don't know the system, and their names are unlikely to appear on vendor lists, on mailing lists of activist organizations, or in multidenominational or multifaith directories. Work through every accessible network to begin to build bridges to them.
10. Bill of Rights. Past practices and assumptions about appropriate church-state relations have left a legacy of distrust between government and faith communities. Government should acknowledge its mistakes and make amends with a statement of the rights of faith-based providers. This would confirm the government's intention to treat them as allies, and it would be a valuable guide to both sides if there is dispute about what actions are permissible.

I was asked to provide expert testimony on the bill in the many committee hearings prior to the vote. I spent hours on research and prepared for each hearing, tailoring my remarks to the specific legislators who would be present. I brought other community experts with me and coached them on how to deliver their testimony in the most effective way. After two years of advocating and lobbying on behalf of this bill, the sponsor retired from public office and the bill died—or so I thought.

A few months later, in preparation for the next session, I scheduled a short meeting with a legislator to inform him of the work my organization was performing in his district. Without any expectations, I outlined how we were serving the at-risk youth in his neighborhoods and how we were partnering with several churches of different denominations to improve the quality of life for his lower-income constituents.

After about ten minutes, he asked me about the fate of the faith-based bill that had been introduced in the prior two sessions of the legislature. I explained that the bill had no champion because the original sponsor had retired. To my great surprise, this second-year representative expressed interest in picking up the bill and trying to push it through in the coming session. He had read the bill and my testimony and served on a committee where the bill could logically be reintroduced. Of course, it helped that this man was a person of faith.

The moral of this story is that you never know from where help will come. Act with due diligence, and you will be rewarded when you least expect it. I am already working toward educating the necessary legislators on this bill before they actually begin their session. That way, they are prepared when the document shows up in their committee and they are fully informed on its pros and cons. They will trust me as an expert witness once again, recognize the bill as beneficial to their constituents, and pass it into law.

LOBBYING VERSUS ADVOCACY

Many people believe that nonprofit organizations are not permitted under any circumstances to lobby public officials for their specific cause. Many have the impression that if they so much as call a public official, their nonprofit status is in jeopardy. This is not accurate. The rules are complicated and require licensed legal counsel. But let's look at what the IRS has published and clear up the uncertainty.

The general rule states that 501(c)(3) corporations may spend up to 20 percent of the first $500,000 of their operating budget, or $100,000, on lobbying. After that initial amount, the percentage changes slightly. If an operating budget is above $500,000, add to the original amount 15 percent of the second $500,000 of the budget. If a budget amounts to more than $1 million, add 10 percent of allowable spending on the third portion. The percentage refers to salary paid to professional lobbyists, printed materials, TV commercials, and any other type of public relations effort a special-interest group might use to sway public opinion.

The two types of lobbying you should know about are direct and grassroots lobbying. *Direct lobbying* happens when a representative of your organization makes a point of telling an elected official or a government employee with influence over legislation what your organization's position on an issue is and asking the official to vote in your favor. It must be specific legislation and a specific opinion expressed to qualify as direct lobbying.

In *grassroots lobbying,* a representative of your organization tries to persuade the general public to voice your position on an issue in an effort to influence legislation. If you are presenting a "call to action" on a particular piece of legislation and asking the public to support your position in correspondence, meetings, or any other type of communication with lawmakers, you are engaging in grassroots lobbying.

The amount a nonprofit may spend on grassroots lobbying is one-quarter the amount it may spend on direct lobbying. So if the annual amount allowed for lobbying is $100,000, only $25,000 could be spent on grassroots lobbying activities. That $25,000 might purchase the skills of an experienced lobbyist for a period of time during a legislative session. The remaining $75,000 could then be spent on direct lobbying methods.

501(H) ELECTION

There has always been a certain amount of ambiguity regarding nonprofit lobbying rules. In 1976, Congress passed the so-called Lobby Law, which allows nonprofit corporations to "elect" to lobby and thus cover themselves from the fear of endangering their status due to lobbying activity. This decision to elect to lobby does not cost the organization any money. A simple one-page form may be downloaded from the IRS Web site at no cost. This step is a safety catch that protects your organization from personal penalties in the event of overspending on lobbying. Another benefit from filing a 501(h) form is that you are less likely to lose tax-exempt status because the IRS may only revoke that status from electing organizations that exceed their lobbying limits by at least 50 percent averaged over a four-year period.

This seems overly complicated; but it is the cost of doing business as a nonprofit. I believe that the benefits outweigh the cost of investigating all the legal ramifications of lobbying. (All this information and more can be found at the Web site of Charity Lobbying in the Public Interest, www.clpi.org.)

To sum up the matter of lobbying, here are a couple of examples.

When the pastor of a church preaches a sermon on client-clergy confidentiality and asks the members of the congregation to call their representatives to express their opposition to a pending bill, that would be direct lobbying. The pastor is asking his members to voice a particular point of view on pending legislation in the hope of influencing the lawmakers' vote.

If Focus on the Family airs a radio broadcast on the issue of parental notification (for girls seeking an abortion) and asks the general public to call congressional representatives and ask them to vote a certain way, that would be considered grassroots lobbying.

Now, if your organization runs an advertisement describing the conditions among the county's homeless population and mentioning the lack of funding for local shelters in the county budget but not specifically asking the public do anything, it is not lobbying at all and so your organization need not be concerned about how much it spent on that ad.

Once you have spent some time learning the ins and outs of government processes, even if you only attend committee hearings as an observer, you are in a much better position to take the next steps of certifying and licensing your organization for government partnerships (if this is appealing to your board).

But what if your organization or program has a smaller budget, which is likely? Does the law mean that you cannot try to sway public opinion if your budget is under $500,000? No. It simply attempts to prevent special-interest groups from gaining too much power over elected officials.

What is more likely in your case—and in fact much more effective—is using volunteers and community partners to influence public policy and opinion. People who don't accept money for their efforts do not have to worry about the complicated legal issues surrounding lobbying and advocacy. Public officials and legislators know that paid lobbyists represent a narrow constituency, but the real power of public opinion is found in passionate, committed volunteers. This will become an increasingly hot topic as the Faith-Based and Community Initiative gains acceptance. We will undoubtedly see more guidelines on this issue in the coming years.

So unless your organization grows at a tremendous rate and has funds to redirect from service to lobbying, this is probably not a problem you need to lose sleep over.

The next chapter deals with that precise matter: assessing your readiness for more serious partnerships and evaluating the quality and results of your work. Evaluation is really the capstone of your social ministry. Even if you get off to a slow start, the slightest attempt to measure your results demonstrates courage and a desire to be better. Keep going! You're almost there.

chapter
EIGHT

Certification and Evaluation

The Importance of Measuring Your Results

No one wants to work for nothing. In the case of ministry, some people would say that they work for the salvation of souls, and that is, of course, a worthy reason to labor. But this chapter deals with the concept of measuring the effects of your work in order to gain professional credibility, funding, an expanded client base, a higher caliber of board member, and many earthly concerns that are necessary for a successful social ministry. All these concerns contribute to the overall success of your work—they afford you the opportunities to help those you want to help in very tangible ways. The exercises in this chapter will walk you through the certification and evaluation processes in a way that will set your work up for maximum service opportunities and partnerships.

Remember the little detail about most of the federal funding for services ending up in the control of the states? Along with that control comes state requirements for most social services that tax dollars support. These requirements vary from state to state, but most states have some sort of expectation that you and your organization have gone through a credentialing process that ensures that you know what you are doing.

Just as a teacher must be trained, pass a test, and earn a credential, an organization must prove that it is qualified to carry out and perform its activities according to a standard that is defined by a related state agency. In the case of education, parochial and private schools need to become accredited by their state if they want their students to receive a diploma from the state and their graduates to attend college.

LICENSING AND CERTIFICATION

Today, many social ministries are choosing to jump through the hoops to become *licensed.* Depending on the area of service, this process is almost mandatory if the ministry wants to be considered for a government grant. And for an organization to become licensed, it is normally required to have a staff that is *certified by the state.* Certification can be a lengthy, arduous experience, again, depending on the area of service.

Do you need a license and certification? This is the first question to ask if you are seeking a government grant. Some service areas are stringent on this matter; others are more lenient. For example, if you run an adult day care program in your home and want to attract families using Medicare, Social Security, or disability insurance, you probably do need to be licensed and certified by the state. If you run a children's day care and want to provide care for low-income families, you probably need to be licensed in your state to qualify for state vouchers.

But if you or your church offers after-school or summer enrichment or tutoring for low-income families, you may not need to be fully licensed as a facility. Many states honor a program that has been designed by a certified schoolteacher who is responsible for training volunteers and mentors. Or perhaps your program has a long-standing agreement with a public school district and is thus "grandfathered in" as qualified due to the history of the relationship.

The simple definition is this: *people become certified* to perform a particular task or function. *An organization becomes licensed* to contract with a government agency (federal, state, or county) for services that the government agency purchases on behalf of others. Sometimes it is enough that an organization has a certified professional in the role of manager, and formal licensure may be waived. Sometimes an organization may become licensed based on its reputation, past performance, or track record, regardless of the level of education or professional experience of its management.

Keep in mind that there may be more than one state agency that needs to sign off or approve your facility. In my state of Washington, any facility that endeavors to contract with the state must also get a green light from the Health Department. So there may be state agencies you don't even know about that you need to satisfy.

VOUCHERS

Voucher systems are in place in many states as a means of distributing Temporary Aid to Needy Families (TANF) funding to eligible families in need. A voucher is simply a coupon that is issued to a person or family to be redeemed at a program of the recipient's choice. Currently, vouchers are used primarily for child care. Some states have also implemented a voucher system for substance abuse treatment. Recipients of TANF help can ask for part of that assistance to be in the form of child care vouchers so that the parent or guardian can select a care provider independent of a case worker's recommendation or approval.

I have it on good authority that the goal of federal agencies is for many more social services to be provided by means of vouchers.

If this system is widely implemented, it would allow clients to choose a service program regardless of whether that program is recognized as acceptable by the state or not.

Of course, this has huge implications for ministries: it could allow any social ministry to participate in the government welfare system without adapting to each state's subjective regulations. Each organization could operate as it normally would, without jumping through certification and licensure hoops, because clients would choose the organization "as is" based on their individual understanding and appreciation of that organization's effectiveness.

So if grandma had her heart set on moving into the Autumn Valley Retirement Home sponsored by her church, her Social Security dollars would *follow her,* instead of *directing her* to acceptable homes deemed worthy by the state.

Note that vouchers have met with success in a few states, but many people bitterly oppose them. One reason this logical solution has bumped up against so much opposition is easy to figure out. Most states receive lots of extra dollars requiring programs and organizations to become licensed and maintain their state's license (or tax). It can be a cash cow for states to set up a system whereby organizations or businesses must periodically alter or update their practices according to what some consider to be arbitrary state regulations.

Another reason the voucher system has not caught on as quickly as many had hoped is because it would require a new plan for distributing, tracking, and redeeming the coupons that would ideally be consistent in each state, as well as with the federal agencies. Everyone knows that changing government systems is like turning the *Queen Mary*! It's no small task.

Does this explanation mean that all state guidelines are arbitrary and unnecessary? No, of course not. Reasonable expectations must be established in order to ensure safety and protection for both the client and the organization. But sometimes we can have too much of a good thing. And in the case of incorporating a new segment of potential contractors, typical state agencies don't see enough benefit for their already stretched resources.

OBTAINING A STATE LICENSE

The fallback position for you who are investigating the possibilities of government partnerships is to *ask lots of questions.* When you think you have exhausted all the questions you can think of, ask someone in the know, "What question should I have asked that I didn't know to ask?" To reiterate, if the voucher system is implemented, much of the hassle of state licensure and certification for many social ministries would go away. We just don't know when that will be.

If you decide to pursue certification and licensure for your organization or church, be aware that the process could take two years or more. You may be in a good position now to start the ball rolling in that direction if you are just getting started. You can save yourself frustration if you make some appointments and find the right people to advise you at the beginning of your formation, rather than after you think you have all the pieces in place. Pick up the phone and start punching numbers. Don't rely on others to tell you all you need to know. They don't know what you don't know, so *ask lots of questions!*

Once you have visited your state's Web site and found the appropriate contact person's name and e-mail or phone number, begin the journey. It is always a good idea to find a licensed organization that is already doing what you want to do, with minor differences. Investigate; make an appointment with the director and arm yourself with pages of questions to ask and lunch for at least the two of you.

Here is a list of questions you might ask during such a site visit:

How long have you been licensed?

How many of your staff are certified?

How have requirements changed over the years you have been in business?

How much do you pay in indirect costs each month (for benefits and the like)?

How much does your annual fee or license cost?

What other unexpected costs do you pay?

Do you carry malpractice insurance?

How are you compensated under your contract (reimbursement or otherwise)?

Do you have to reapply each year?

What is the cost of the application?

Are your staff members required to earn continuing education credits?

Who pays for that?

Does your government contract cover your entire budget?

How are your costs reassessed each year?

What are the penalties for contract violations?

What kind of reporting are you responsible for?

How many staff do you dedicate for reporting and evaluation?

If you had it to do over again, would you contract with the state?

What are the hazards of state contracting?

What do I need to know if I am planning on starting the process of licensure?

As usual, take good notes, and keep a file on all you learn. Pay close attention to the folks who treat you well and encourage you. You'll want to continue to use them as a resource every step of the way. They could be a potential board member or adviser down the road.

OUTCOME-BASED EVALUATION

The first time I heard of outcome-based evaluation, I assumed it was the same thing as outcome-based education, and consequently, I wanted nothing to do with it! It turns out that it is similar in ways but also different. The bottom line is that outcome-based evaluation is a necessary and beneficial practice that will improve the way any business or organization functions. It is not, as some believe, an extra layer of unnecessary bureaucracy intending to discourage the uninitiated.

As I've already mentioned, years ago, grants were awarded by foundations, corporations, and government agencies with little follow-up or accountability required of the grantee. The consequences are still leaving marks today. The 1990s was a decade of facing the truth for many government agencies and lawmakers. Welfare reform included new strategies such as the Paperwork Reduction Act and the Personal Responsibility Act. Runaway budgets with questionable results prompted funders to demand "measurable outcomes" from the nonprofits they supported. Outcome-based evaluation was born!

Today, every request for proposal (RFP) or request for application (RFA) (see Chapter Six) or foundation and corporate funding announcement asks for a detailed description of how the proposed project will be evaluated for effectiveness. It is usually the final item in an RFP, but it always carries the weight of at least 10 percent of the overall quality of the proposal. Evaluation is thus something to take seriously and understand very well before you devise your plan.

Let's assume you don't intend to submit grant proposals at all, based on the information you gleaned from Chapter Four. Let's assume that you and your team intend to raise your budget by appealing to friends, churches, and small businesses that you frequent regularly. Is evaluation still such a big deal? Yes, if you want to expand your services and continue to attract new support.

Here's why: in our increasingly sophisticated society, people who give money away are no longer satisfied with the good feeling they get when they send in their check to the local food bank. Today, folks are aware of business fraud, "cooked books," inflated stocks, and generally shoddy management. We have seen it on TV every night for the past few years. It has left a bad taste in the mouth of the average American. People are still willing to part with their hard-earned cash, but they want to see evidence of the value their investment is building.

That evidence is produced through outcome-based evaluation. It is a brilliant method to both guide the process of measuring effectiveness and demonstrate tangible results. The beauty is that any program, project, department, or household can implement the method. There is virtually no limit to what you can measure once you learn the technique. Keep in mind that most professional evaluators have been prepared in this medium with at least one graduate-level course. Recent years have given us a handful of exceptional trainers in the practice of evaluation that may be found in universities, policy think tanks, and larger nonprofit organizations. I recently attended a conference of the American Evaluators Association that had an international audience of about fifteen hundred people. Outcome-based evaluation has become a scientific discipline similar to statistics or accounting. Major university schools of sociology and public policy now offer doctorates in evaluation. (Some names and contact information are listed on our Web site, www.josseybass.com/go/esau.) An excellent introductory tool is the book *Outcomes for Success!* by Jane Reisman and Judith Clegg.

THE LOGIC MODEL

A common tool used in outcome-based evaluation is known as—the *logic model.* You will learn to create you own logic model, but first let's discuss some of the theory. I like to think of the process as a logical description of the model I am seeking to form.

Outcome-based evaluation means identifying the precise items and methods you will use to determine if you are accomplishing your goals. You state these items and methods up front so that you can track your progress and make corrections along the way. This will become clearer as we work through the model step by step (four sample logic models are presented in Exhibits 8.1 through 8.4).

Exhibit 8.1
Sample Logic Model: Midwest Compassion, Year One

Participant: Capacity Center

Goal: An integrated and more peaceful society in which to live and raise healthy families (which brings honor and glory to God)

Activities	Outputs	Outcomes
Set up central office	Hire three staff people to open an office	A viable network of faith-based nonprofit organizations fully prepared to partner with complementary groups and government agencies at any level for a variety of services
Act as adviser and information broker to faith-based organizations, government, and secular nonprofits	Create and publish a comprehensive database and matrix	Elevated capacity within grassroots FBOs allowing for increased quality and quantity of service
Build capacity in grassroots FBOs	Hold forty "brown-bag" training sessions	Improved communication throughout the social service sector via an interactive Web site
Maintain an interactive Web site	Conduct twenty-five on-site evaluations	Increased self-sufficiency in urban and rural populations
Build local, state, and national collaborations	Sponsor two statewide events featuring national FBO or government leaders	Reduction in generational welfare
Sponsor training sessions	Establish ten new collaborations	Greater awareness and treatment of societal ills through volunteer "armies of compassion"
Develop resources on behalf of the entire alliance	Develop a comprehensive list of projects and FBOs ready to collaborate	
Represent FBOs' interests in economic and political matters when appropriate		
Develop and publish evaluation tools specific to FBOs		

Completion Date: 75 percent of the items mentioned would be in full operation by Sept. 2007 (assuming a funding date of Oct. 2005)

Exhibit 8.2
Sample Logic Model: SHARE Program

Participant: SHARE Program

Goal: To substantially increase the number and scope of the SHARE program, leading to a decrease in teen sexual activity and healthier relationships

Activities	Outputs	Outcomes
Teach abstinence education to junior high and high school students nationwide	Establish SHARE partners in 150 school districts across the country and internationally	Reduced sexual activity among teens domestically and abroad
Train volunteers to present the proven curricula	Graduate 300 trained presenters in the same targeted areas	Reduced teen pregnancy
Track effectiveness of the program regionally and nationally	Present the SHARE message and materials to 75,000 students in the first contract year	Reduced teen abortions
Advise and participate in school and community marketing efforts	Generate and publish 150 district reports revealing the results of student surveys	Reduced teen cases of sexually transmitted diseases
Develop mentor relationships with partner schools	Conduct an annual follow-up and publish a report	Reduced numbers of teen runaways and teen homeless
		Improved physical and emotional health among teens
		More stable family situations among teens
		Improved school performance
		Reduced medical and insurance costs

Completion Date: Apr. 2007 (assuming a funding date of Oct. 2005)

Exhibit 8.3
Sample Logic Model: Finance Department

Participant: Finance Department

Goal: Maintenance of sound financial health for the organization

Resources	Activities	Outputs	Outcomes
Board of directors	Hold monthly meetings	Conduct four or five fundraising projects over the course of the year	Streamlined financial matters
Finance committee	Formulate and propose budgets	Reconcile financial statements monthly	Balanced books at start of each fiscal year
Staff	File quarterly reports	Approve any expense over $300	Improved business practices
Bank personnel	Propose and support all fundraising efforts	Countersign all payroll checks	Unhindered growth
Funding entities	Recruit volunteer to perform annual audit	Audit the department monthly	More widespread reputation
Families paying tuition		Increase revenues in preparation for expansion	Increased funding

Exhibit 8.4
Sample Logic Model: Project Digital Divide, Phase One

Goals:

- Healthier communities based on a structure of stable families with unlimited educational and economic opportunities
- A common sense of pride and contentment among a traditionally stressed population, resulting in shared resources and mutual support
- A demonstration that effective systems and outcomes result when local entities work together for the collective good

Resources	Activities	Outputs	Outcomes
Staff: management, tutors and trainers, volunteers, facilitators, evaluators	Secure funding and support for communitywide technology training project	Conduct five hours of computer and Internet training per day per site	Increased efficiency in neighborhood organizations providing education and social services
Facilities: 13 organizations, 10 sites, secured buildings (geographically spread, well maintained)	Select sites for training	Conduct training sessions at ten sites in three low-income areas of the city	New funding streams attracted to target neighborhoods through the success of this project
Equipment: computers, printers, Internet access	Recruit volunteers	Conduct training sessions over a one-year period under foundation grant	Job placement for the unemployed
Funding partners: (6)	Recruit participants	Train four hundred participants in one year at the ten sites	Promotion for the employed
Other: school district	Design curricula	Test each participant for progress and acumen once a week	Peer leadership emerging from this communitywide effort
	Obtain computers		
	Install computers		
	Install Internet access		
	Establish evaluation methods and criteria		
	Conduct training sessions		

Exhibit 8.4
Sample Logic Model: Project Digital Divide, Phase One, Cont'd.

Resources	Activities	Outputs	Outcomes
	Hold weekly meetings	Track progress at each site with forms provided	More interdependent relationships among schools, businesses, community groups, churches, government, and families
	Report on progress	Post monthly reports on the Web site for maximum exposure	Improved academic performance in schoolchildren through twelfth grade
	Adjust outputs and outcomes as necessary		Better home life for the working poor
	Interview participants		Increased income for all participants
	Solicit feedback		More students seeking higher education
	Administer tests		
	Document observations		

Step 1: Specify Your Goal

I like to begin this exercise with the end goal first because it helps us remember why we are working so hard. What are we trying to accomplish, and how will the world be better as a result of our work? Achieving your goal usually takes help from others. If you are attempting to "end the spread of HIV/AIDS in the African American population," you will need to ask many others to join you. Your goal should be big. Notice that you may have more than one goal. If you are working in an existing program, you may have more than one program or direct service area or service, in which case you may have two or three goals listed, but the processes used to accomplish those goals are the same as if you had selected one major goal.

Once you are certain of what you are trying to do, you can begin to analyze how to get there.

Step 2: List All Your Resources

This step is always surprising for first-time logic model drafters. There are obvious things most people include right away, like money, facilities, and transportation. But try to think broadly here: your students or constituents are a resource because they spread the news about the project. Your equipment is a resource because it allows you to do your work. Your local government is a great resource, even if you haven't used it as such yet. Try to exhaust you resource options; they will provide more creative ways to do your work, as you will see.

Some logic model trainers eliminate this step if they are working with an experienced organization that has been through the process before. It is fine to adapt your model to fit your organizational needs. In fact, when you begin to look at RFPs, each evaluation or logic model section will vary slightly. It is good to be aware of them now so that you will not be confused when you actually read through differing RFPs. Just address the categories listed in the RFP, and give the sponsoring agency exactly what is being asked for.

Step 3: Identify All Your Activities

To help yourself come up with all the things you do, it's easiest to think of what you do by week, month, and year. You don't need to separate the time categories on your logic model, unless you find that helpful. But most service providers forget all of the small yet important tasks and meetings they manage during the course of a month. Each one can be very significant when you are describing your work to a potential funder. Think of how relationships are built with youth over four Wednesday night pizza feeds. So, ask your team questions like these:

- What is it our youth program does every week? (meetings, outreach, Bible studies, pizza night, mentoring of middle school students, and so on)
- What do we do as monthly activities? (attend a concert, community service project, leading worship on Sunday night, and so on)
- What happens in our youth program once a year? (spring or summer camp, outreach night with a professional athlete, food drive for the homeless, and so on)

This list will probably also surprise you. It is very inspiring when you actually write down in one place all the work your group actually does. These activities are very important because they are usually the vehicle through which your "outcomes" are processed.

Step 4: Quantify Your Activity (Outputs)

How much of everything is being done? Calculate numbers for your actions to show how much of everything is being done; for example:

Activity	Outputs
Middle school tutoring	20 kids tutored twice a week
Middle school mentoring	12 kids mentored one day a week
Outreach pizza night	50 new kids once a month
Community service	15 students clean six senior units

This list should be as long as possible because your outcomes will derive from it.

Note that some evaluators include another category here, developed as a separate list, the indicators list.

Indicators simply name what precise tool you will use to determine your measures. For example, if you are evaluating the youth program, you may use camp sign-ups as an indicator of getting the word out about the camp. You may also use classroom test scores as an indicator that your academic tutoring is having a positive effect (producing outcomes) on the middle school kids. Some evaluators develop an indicator list for each outcome. This draws a clear line from results back to how those claims may be supported. Some evaluators include indicators in their outcomes list—for example, "80 percent of tutored middle schoolers will improve math test scores by one grade level."

Step 5: Calculate Your Outcomes

The outcomes list is where the rubber meets the road. It is the data you publish in your annual report and what you talk about when you are seeking funding or other types of support. Here is where you establish whether or not your work is having an impact and producing results. Don't forget, outcomes are what your volunteers, funders, and board members are investing toward—you must show outcomes to keep everyone coming back and to attract new partners.

Using your previous categories of resources, activities, and outputs, answer the question "What have we caused to change as a result of what we do?" You will want to use words such as *increase, decrease, improve, reduce, elevate,* and *diminish.*

Outputs	**Outcomes**
20 kids tutored twice a week	Math and reading scores improve
	Students respect the teacher more
	Family relationships are stabilized and thrive
50 new students attend pizza night	Youth violence is decreased
	Trusting relationships are established
	Teen sexual activity is decreased
	Teen employment is increased
	Crime is reduced, making for safer streets

These types of outcomes can be measured by police records, hospital emergency room numbers, labor statistics, and many more indicators in the public domain. Measurable outcomes are expected from faith-based and secular nonprofits if they are to be trusted with clients' needs, donors' dollars, and community partnerships. So as you think through the process of program evaluation, make sure you train yourself and your staff to ask the right questions that will lead you to the kind of outcomes your stakeholders identify with. You don't want to be like the painter who completed half his job only to find out his ladder was leaning against the wrong wall!

Don't be discouraged if you don't get the perfect logic model outline on your first attempt. This exercise takes practice. You'll get better the more times you work through it. (You might want to use Worksheet 8.1; make as many copies as you need.) Sometimes a simple client and volunteer survey of your work can tell you what you should be measuring and how that data could best be collected.

Client surveys are widely used, fairly reliable tools that let you know how effective your work is. If you're really brave, you'll include a question inviting the responder to comment on an issue you have not addressed in your survey. This will really tell you what you should be asking and measuring. A sample conference evaluation is presented in Exhibit 8.5.

As with most of the material covered in this book, there is plenty of room for revision and adaptation even after you have a printed document in your hand. It is always a good idea to revisit your logic model and program evaluation tools periodically because clients and conditions change. If you are doing a good job, you will probably begin to expand and grow. Growth is a great outcome to announce to the world.

But let's not forget the nature of our ministry; shouldn't we all be trying to work ourselves out of a job? Yes, the poor will always be with us, and the human condition is less than it was designed to be. But let's not lose sight of our vision, our preferred future. Let's continue to hold fast to the promise that good has overcome evil. The outcomes we pursue are not just to expand our ministry. They are to relieve the pain and suffering we observe around us every day. If we are doing our job well, hurting hearts will confess, one by one, "There is a God in Heaven!" because they will see our good deeds performed in His name.

Worksheet 8.1

Logic Model Worksheet

Organization/Participant/Program: ______________________

Goal: ______________________

Resources	Activities	Outputs	Outcomes

Exhibit 8.5
Faith-Based Conference Workshop Evaluation

Name (optional): ______________________________

1. How did you hear about this event? (Circle all that apply.)

   E-mail   Phone   Work contact   Friend

2. How useful was the information presented today? (Circle all that apply.)

   Extremely useful   Moderately useful   Not useful

3. Will your organization pursue state certification contracts?

   Yes   Don't know yet   No

4. Which workshop discussion did you like best?

   Certification and licensure   Contracting   Evaluation

5. Would you be interested in attending other workshops? If so, in which areas? (Circle all that apply.)

Substance abuse	Mental health	Education
Justice issues	Labor	Faith-based organizations
Transitional housing	Homelessness	Advocacy
Government relations	Grantwriting	Nonprofit Administration

   Other ______________________________

6. How could we improve this event next time?

   ____

   ____

Conclusion

Where Do You Go from Here?

Congratulations! You have persevered. You have used the worksheets and followed the guidelines, and you now have some solid groundwork under your feet. You have assessed the need you feel called to meet. You understand your client or constituent base better by analyzing your stakeholders list. You know your strengths, weaknesses, opportunities, and threats. You have a good idea of your mission, vision, and values statements, so you will avoid spinning your wheels.

Your board of directors and your advisory board are reflecting and promoting your values, but you now know not to rush into commitments with these relationships. However you feel about finances and budgets, you now at least understand how important they are to your success and performance, as well as your ability to raise sufficient funds to operate your nonprofit business. And you keep the requisite knowledge and expertise at your fingertips by surrounding yourself with competent advisers.

You have been shown how to treat volunteers and have thought about where and when to set up shop. Perhaps you have even attempted some grantwriting. But you now understand that acquiring government dollars in support of your work is not a simple process. Nevertheless, you can approach any public official with confidence and introduce your work with clarity. This new clarity should be based on solid data collected through valid evaluation measures. Don't despair if it seems that you'll never complete the full picture you want to see. There must be joy in the journey; part of that joy is knowing that you have been obedient to God, following your call. Part of the joy is bringing others along with you so that they can pick up the torch and carry on alongside you or after you have given all you have to give. True servants do not grow weary in doing good; we persevere until the appropriate time, when we will reap our reward. Don't give up!

If you already had a working organization before you picked up this book, you now have some information that will help you take your service to the next level. You can go back, page by page, and review your notes, summarize what helped you most, and set the book on a nearby shelf for frequent reference. You may even want to pass a copy along to a colleague or friend.

Don't be discouraged if you *haven't* set your operations up according to the "best practices" presented here. It is never too late to adapt or tweak existing procedures. In fact, certain types of change can infuse an organization with new life and energy. Times of change can be the best moments to attract new partners and investors. Reinventing an image shows an ability to grow and respond to current needs around you.

Where you go from here is up to you. You now have some decisions to make: Are you ready to move forward with your plans? Should you pursue certification and licensing? With whom would you like to partner? What should you do next about fundraising? Can you attempt to write a government grant proposal? I suggest that you do one more exercise: write down all your questions, and discuss your next steps with your team. Do it in a creative way—have a party!

My final words of advice to you soldiers in the army of compassion are to *celebrate your small victories.* Go out tonight and celebrate finishing this book. Bring along a friend, colleague, family member, anyone who will understand just how important your ministry is to you. Get in the habit of recognizing how significant even the smallest accomplishments are when you are serving the Lord. Commit all decisions to prayer and then listen for His response. Never embark on a path without a clear and distinct go from God, then from your advisers, and finally from your circumstances. If those three line up, you have a solid indication on which way to go.

To close this book, I ask you, my partner in service, for a special favor: please send me your feedback on what you have read and let me know what you intend to do with the information contained in this book. There will be much more to share in the coming months as more and more social ministry outcomes are reported. The reelection of President Bush and his administration will almost certainly have a significant effect on the future of government–faith-based and community partnerships. There is already talk of reintroducing the original faith-based bill that was proposed to Congress in 2001. And new opportunities may arise. What will it mean, and how should we in the faith community respond to these potential changes? Your feedback will help me decide if I should attempt another volume addressing these policy issues or write one for specific areas of service, such as substance abuse programs, out-of-school care partnerships, or juvenile justice strategies. My decision and the decision of my editors will be based on the feedback we get from readers like you. So hop onto www.josseybass.com/go/esau and leave your comments.

Until then, I send you my sincere gratitude for what you are doing on behalf of so many neighbors in need. You are the glue that binds society together. You are the only hope that the despairing may see. You are the reflection of the bright and morning star, fulfilling exactly what you were designed to do. Thank you. You have heard your call, and you are answering in the best way you know how. What could be better than that?

resource
A

ARTICLES OF INCORPORATION OF WEEKEND CONFERENCES NORTHWEST

The undersigned, acting as the incorporator of a nonprofit corporation under the provisions of RCW 24.03, adopts the following Articles of Incorporation for such corporation.

ARTICLE I: NAME

The name of this corporation is Weekend Conferences Northwest.

ARTICLE II: DURATION

The existence of this corporation shall be perpetual.

ARTICLE III: PURPOSE

1. This corporation is organized and operated exclusively for religious, charitable, and educational purposes within the meaning of Section 501(c)(3) of the Internal Revenue Code of 1986, as amended, or the corresponding provision of any further United States internal revenue law or successor statute ("Code"). Consistent with and subject to its qualification under Section 501(c)(3) of the Code, the corporation is organized and operated to unify, equip, and enable faith-based organizations to serve their communities more effectively, to assist with providing resources to help faith-based organizations expand and grow, and to conduct any other lawful activity permitted under the laws of the State of Washington.

2. No part of the net earnings of the corporation shall inure to the benefit of any private shareholder or individual.

3. No substantial part of the activities of the corporation shall be the carrying on of propaganda, or otherwise attempting to influence legislation (except as otherwise provided in Section 501(h) of the Code).

4. The corporation shall not participate in, or intervene in (including the publishing or distributing of statements) any political campaign on behalf of (or in opposition to) any candidate for public office, all within the meaning of Section 501(c)(3) of the Code.

ARTICLE IV: POWERS

The corporation shall have all powers granted by law necessary and proper to carry out its above-stated purposes, consistent with its qualification under Section 501(c)(3) of the Code.

ARTICLE V: BYLAWS

Provisions for the regulation of the internal affairs of the corporation shall be set forth in the bylaws.

ARTICLE VI: FULL TAX BENEFIT

In the event this corporation is classified as a private foundation, the corporation's officers intend to maintain the full benefit of tax exemption to which the corporation may be entitled under the Code. Accordingly, the corporation shall be managed in a manner consistent with the officers' intent. Without limiting the generality of the foregoing, in the event of such classification, the corporation shall

1. Distribute its income for each taxable year at such time and in such manner as not to subject the corporation to tax under Section 4942 of the Code.
2. Not engage in any action of self-dealing as defined in Section 4941(d) of the Code.
3. Not retain any excess business holdings as defined in Section 4943(c) of the Code.

4. Not make any investment that jeopardizes the corporation's charitable purposes as defined in Section 4944 of the Code.

5. Not make any taxable expenditures as defined in Section 4945(d) of the Code.

ARTICLE VII: DIRECTOR LIABILITY

To the full extent that Washington law, as it exists on the date hereof or may hereafter be amended, permits the limitation or elimination of the liability of directors, a director of this corporation shall not be liable to this corporation for monetary damages for conduct as a director. Any amendments to or repeal of this Article VII shall not adversely affect any right or protection of a director of this corporation for or with respect to any acts or omissions of such director occurring prior to such amendment or repeal.

ARTICLE VIII: INDEMNIFICATION

This corporation has the power to indemnify (including the power to advance expenses to) its directors, officers, employees, and agents made a party to a proceeding, as defined in the Washington Business Corporation Act, without regard to the limitations in RCW 23B.08.510 through 23B.08.550; provided, however, that no such indemnity shall indemnify any such director, officer, employee, or agent from or on account of (1) acts or omissions of such director, officer, employee, or agent finally adjudged to be intentional misconduct or a knowing violation of law; (2) conduct of the director, officer, employee, or agent finally adjudged to be in violation of RCW 23B.08.310; or (3) any transaction with respect to which it was finally adjudged that such director, officer, employee, or agent personally received a benefit in money, property, or services to which such person was not legally entitled.

ARTICLE IX: DISTRIBUTION UPON DISSOLUTION

In the event of dissolution, the net assets of the corporation shall be distributed only to a recipient or recipients, to be selected by the Board of Directors, that would qualify for exemption as an organization described in Section 501(c)(3) of the Code. Provided, however, notwithstanding the foregoing, if the corporation is classified as a private foundation as defined in Section 509 of the Code, and if its status as a private foundation is terminated pursuant to Section 507(a) of the Code, and Sections

507(b) or 507(g)(2) are inapplicable, all the net assets of the corporation shall be distributed to one or more organizations selected by the Board of Directors and described in Section 170(b)(1)(A) of the Code (other than in clauses vii and viii), each of which has been in existence and so described for a continuous period of at least 60 calendar months. However, this proviso shall only apply if the Secretary of the Department of the Treasury of the United States of America abates any tax imposed on the corporation by reason of Section 507(c) of the Code pursuant to the abatement authority granted the Secretary by Section 507(g) of the Code.

ARTICLE X: REGISTERED OFFICE AND AGENT

The address of the initial registered office of the corporation is 500 Union Street, Seattle, WA 98101, and the name of its initial registered agent at such address is John Jacobs, Attorney at Law.

ARTICLE XI: INITIAL DIRECTORS

The number of directors constituting the initial Board of Directors of the corporation is five, and the names and addresses of the persons who are to serve as the initial directors are as follows:

Name	**Address**
____________________	____________________
____________________	____________________
____________________	____________________
____________________	____________________
____________________	____________________

ARTICLE XII: INCORPORATOR

The incorporator is John Jacobs, and his address is 500 Union Street, Seattle, WA 98101.

EXECUTED in duplicate in Seattle, Washington, this _____ day of January, 2003.

____

John Jacobs, Incorporator

resource
B

BYLAWS OF WEEKEND CONFERENCES NORTHWEST

ARTICLE I: BOARD OF DIRECTORS

Section 1 There shall be no members of this corporation.

Section 2 The management and administration of the affairs of this corporation shall be by a self-perpetuating Board of Directors consisting of not less than three persons, who shall serve terms of one year each and until their successors are elected and qualified.

Section 3 Within the limits of Section 2 hereof, the number of directors may be changed at any time by a majority vote of the directors present at any regular meeting or at any special meeting called in whole or in part for that purpose.

Section 4 One-half of the members of the Board of Directors shall constitute a quorum.

Section 5 The Board of Directors may designate and appoint by resolution adopted by majority of the directors one or more committees, each of which shall consist of two or more directors, which committee or committees, to the extent provided in such resolution, shall have and exercise the authority of the Board of Directors in the management of the corporation.

Section 6 Any one or more of the directors may be removed at any time by a vote of two-thirds of the directors present at any regular meeting or at any special meeting called in whole or in part for that purpose.

Section 7 In the event of a vacancy on the Board of Directors, the remaining directors by majority vote of the directors present may elect a successor to fill the unexpired term. If there is only one director serving, the director may elect successors to fill the unexpired terms of vacant positions on the Board. If all positions are vacant by reason of death or otherwise, Weekend Conferences USA, Inc., or its designated successor, shall have authority to appoint persons to fill three vacancies, such persons to be selected for their interest and ability to carry out the purposes of the corporation.

Section 8 Any action required or permitted to be taken at a meeting of the Board of Directors may be taken without a meeting if a written consent setting forth the action to be taken is signed by all of the directors. Any such written consent shall be inserted in the minutes book as if it were the minutes of a Board meeting.

ARTICLE II: OFFICERS

Section 1 The elected officers of the corporation shall be a president, one or more vice-presidents, a secretary, a treasurer, and such other officers and assistant officers as may be deemed necessary by the Board of Directors, including a chairman of the Board. Each officer shall be annually elected by the Board and shall serve until a successor is duly elected and qualified. Any two or more offices may be held by the same person, except the offices of president and secretary. In addition to the powers and duties specified below, the officers shall have such powers and perform such duties as the Board of Directors may prescribe.

Section 2 The chairman, if such an officer is elected, shall preside at meetings of the Board of Directors.

Section 3 The president shall exercise the usual executive powers pertaining to the office of president. If there is no chairman of the Board, or if the chairman is absent, the president shall preside at all meetings of the Board of Directors.

Section 4 In the absence or disability of the president, the vice-president shall act as president.

Section 5 It shall be the duty of the secretary to keep records of the proceedings of the Board of Directors, and when requested by the president to do so, to sign and execute with the president all deeds, bonds, contracts, and other obligations, or instruments, in the name of the corporation, to keep the corporate seal, and to affix the same to proper documents.

Section 6 The treasurer shall have the care and custody of and be responsible for all funds and investments of the corporation, and shall cause to be kept regular books of account. The treasurer shall cause to be deposited all funds and other valuable effects in the name of the corporation in such depositories as may be designated by the Board of Directors.

Section 7 Vacancies in any office arising from any cause may be filled by the Board of Directors at any regular or special meeting.

Section 8 The salaries of all officers and agents of the corporation shall be fixed by the Board of Directors.

Section 9 Any officer elected or appointed may be removed by a majority of the Board of Directors whenever in its judgment the best interests of the corporation will be served thereby.

Section 10 Checks from any bank account of the corporation shall be signed only by such officer or officers as the Board of Directors may from time to time appoint by an appropriate resolution.

ARTICLE III: MEETINGS

Section 1 The annual meeting of the Board of Directors shall be held during the month of January, beginning with the year 2004. If in the judgment of the Board of Directors the meeting cannot be then held, it shall be held as soon as feasible thereafter. The Board of Directors may specify by resolution the time and place, either within or without the State of Washington, for holding any regular meetings, which may be held without notice other than such resolution.

Section 2 Special meetings of the directors shall be held upon the call of the president or the chairman or upon the written request and ten (10) days' notice in writing signed by one-third of the Board of Directors. Notice of any meeting of the Board of Directors may be waived in writing by any directors at any time.

Section 3 Each director shall be entitled to cast one vote at any election or on any subject before any meeting of the Board.

ARTICLE IV: CONTROL OF FUNDS

Section 1 The Board of Directors shall have exclusive control and power over all grants, contributions, and other financial assistance made by the corporation, all of which must be in furtherance of the corporation's purposes.

Section 2 The Board of Directors shall have the power to make grants and contributions and otherwise render financial assistance to any organization organized and operated exclusively for exempt purposes as set forth in Section 50l(c)(3) of the Internal Revenue Code of 1986, as amended, or the corresponding provision of any further United States internal revenue law or successor statute, provided such assistance is in furtherance of the corporation's purposes.

Section 3 The Board of Directors shall review all requests for funds from other organizations and require that such requests specify the use to which the funds will be put. Upon approval of the request, payment of the funds may be authorized to that organization.

Section 4 The Board of Directors shall require that an organization that receives funds provide a periodic accounting to show that the funds were expended for the use as approved by the Board of Directors.

Section 5 The Board of Directors may, in its absolute discretion, refuse to make any grants or contributions or otherwise render financial assistance to or for any or all the purposes for which funds are requested.

Section 6 Upon approval of any request as described in Section 3, the Board of Directors may solicit funds for that specific project or purpose, but may at any time exercise its right to withdraw approval and to use the funds received for other religious, charitable, or educational purposes. The Board of Directors shall refuse to accept any contribution that does not allow the corporation complete control and discretion to use funds in furtherance of the corporation's purposes.

ARTICLE V: INDEMNIFICATION OF DIRECTORS, OFFICERS, EMPLOYEES, AND AGENTS

Section 1. Power to Indemnify The corporation shall have the following powers:

Section 1.1. Power to Indemnify The corporation may indemnify and hold harmless to the full extent permitted by applicable law each person who was or is made a party to or is threatened to be made a party to or is involved (including, without limitation, as a witness) in any actual or threatened action, suit, or other proceeding, whether civil, criminal, administrative, or investigative, and whether formal or informal (hereinafter a "proceeding"), by reason of the fact that he or she is or was a director, officer, employee, or agent of the corporation or, being or having been such a director, officer, employee, or agent, he or she is or was serving at the request of the corporation as a director, officer, employee, agent, trustee, or in any other capacity of another corporation or of a partnership, joint venture, trust, or other enterprise, including service with respect to employee benefit plans, whether the basis of such proceeding is alleged action or omission in an official capacity or in any other capacity while serving as a director, officer, employee, agent, trustee, or in any other capacity, against all expense, liability, and loss (including, without limitation, attorneys' fees, judgments, fines, ERISA excise taxes or penalties, and amounts to be paid in settlement) actually or reasonably incurred or suffered by such person in connection therewith. Such indemnification may continue as to a person who has ceased to be a director, officer, employee, or agent of the corporation and shall inure to the benefit of his or her heirs and personal representatives.

Section 1.2. Power to Pay Expenses in Advance of Final Disposition The corporation may pay expenses incurred in defending any proceeding in advance of its final disposition (hereinafter "advancement of expenses"); provided, however, that any advancement of expenses shall be made to or on behalf of a director, officer, employee, or agent only upon delivery to the corporation of (a) a written affirmation of the director's, officer's, employee's, or agent's good faith belief that he or she has met the standard of conduct described in RCW 23B.08.510, and (b) a written undertaking, by or on behalf of such director, officer, employee, or agent, to repay all amounts so advanced if it shall ultimately be determined by final judicial decision from which there is no further right to appeal that such director, officer, employee, or agent is not entitled to be indemnified under this Article or otherwise, which undertaking may be unsecured and may be accepted without reference to financial ability to make repayment.

Section 1.3. Power to Enter into Contracts The corporation may enter into contracts with any person who is or was a director, officer, employee, or agent of the corporation in furtherance of the provisions of this Article and may create a trust fund, grant a security interest in property of the corporation, or use other means (including, without limitation, a letter of credit) to ensure the payment of such amounts as may be necessary to effect indemnification as provided in this Article.

Section 1.4. Expansion of Powers If the Washington Business Corporation Act or the Washington Nonprofit Corporation Act is amended in the future to expand or increase the power of the corporation to indemnify, to pay expenses in advance of final disposition, to enter into contracts, or to expand or increase any similar or related power, then, without any further requirement of action by the directors of this corporation, the powers described in this Article shall be expanded and increased to the fullest extent permitted by the Washington Business Corporation Act and the Washington Nonprofit Corporation Act, as so amended.

Section 1.5. Limitation of Powers No indemnification shall be provided under this Article to any such person if the corporation is prohibited by the Washington Business Corporation Act or other applicable law as then in effect from paying such indemnification. For example, no indemnification shall be provided to any person in respect of any proceeding, whether or not involving action in his or her official capacity, in which he or she shall have been finally adjudged to be liable on the basis of intentional misconduct or knowing violation of law by the person, or from conduct of a director in violation of RCW 23B.08.310, or that the person personally received a benefit in money, property, or services to which the person was not legally entitled.

Section 2. Indemnification of Directors, Officers, Employees and Agents

Section 2.1. Directors The corporation shall indemnify and hold harmless any person who is or was a director of this corporation, and pay expenses in advance of final disposition of a proceeding, to the full extent to which the corporation is empowered.

Section 2.2. Officers, Employees, and Agents The corporation, by action of its Board of Directors, may indemnify and hold harmless any person who is or was an officer, employee, or agent of the corporation, and provide advancement of expenses to the full extent to which the corporation is empowered, or to any lesser extent which the Board of Directors may determine.

Section 2.3. Character of Rights To the extent the rights of indemnification and advancement of expenses have been conferred by or pursuant to this Article, such rights shall be contract rights.

Section 2.4. Enforcement A director ("Claimant") shall be presumed to be entitled to indemnification and/or advancement of expenses under this Article upon submission of a written claim (and, in an action brought to enforce a claim for an advancement of expenses, where the undertaking in subsection 1.2. above has been delivered to the corporation) and thereafter the corporation shall have the burden of proof to overcome the presumption that the Claimant is so entitled.

If a claim under this Article is not paid in full by the corporation within sixty days after a written claim has been received by the corporation, except in the case of a claim for advancement of expenses, in which case the applicable period shall be twenty days, the Claimant may at any time thereafter bring suit against the corporation to recover the unpaid amount of the claim. If successful in whole or in part, the Claimant shall also be entitled to be paid the expense of prosecuting such claim. Neither the failure of the corporation (including its Board of Directors or independent legal counsel) to have made a determination prior to the commencement of such action that indemnification of or advancement of expenses to the Claimant is proper in the circumstances nor an actual determination by the corporation (including its Board of Directors or independent legal counsel) that the Claimant is not entitled to indemnification or advancement of expenses shall be a defense to the action or create a presumption that the Claimant is not so entitled.

Section 2.5. Rights Not Exclusive The right to indemnification and advancement of expenses conferred in this Article shall not be exclusive of any other right which any person may have or hereafter acquire under any statute, provision of the Articles of Incorporation or Bylaws of the corporation, agreement, vote of disinterested directors, or otherwise.

Section 3. Insurance The corporation may purchase and maintain insurance, at its expense, to protect itself and any director, officer, employee, or agent of the corporation or any person who, while a director, officer, employee, or agent of the corporation, is or was a director, officer, partner, trustee, employee, or agent of another corporation, partnership, joint venture, trust, employee benefit plan, or other enterprise against any expense, liability, or loss, whether or not the corporation would have the power to indemnify such person against such expense, liability, or loss under the Washington Business Corporation Act.

Section 4. Survival of Benefits Any repeal or modification of this Article shall not adversely affect any right of any person existing at the time of such repeal or modification.

Section 5. Severability If any provision of this Article or any application thereof shall be invalid, unenforceable, or contrary to applicable law, the remainder of this Article, or the application of such provision to persons or circumstances other than those as to which it is held invalid, unenforceable, or contrary to applicable law, shall not be affected thereby and shall continue in full force and effect.

Section 6. Applicable Law For purposes of this Article, "applicable law" shall at all times be construed as the applicable law in effect at the date indemnification may be sought, or the law in effect at the date of the action, omission, or other event giving rise to the situation for which indemnification may be sought, whichever is selected by the person seeking indemnification.

ARTICLE VI: ADMINISTRATIVE PROVISIONS

Section 1 The fiscal year of the corporation shall be determined by resolution adopted by the Board of Directors. In the absence of such a resolution, the fiscal year shall be the calendar year.

Section 2 No loans shall be made by the corporation to any officer or to any director.

Section 3 These Bylaws may be amended by a two-thirds vote of the directors present at any regular meeting of the Board, provided that the directors were notified before the meeting that an amendment or amendments would be considered at the meeting.

The undersigned, being the secretary of the corporation, hereby certifies that these Bylaws consisting of _______ pages are the Bylaws of the Corporation, adopted by resolution of the directors on ____________________, 2003.

DATED this ______ day of ________________, 2003.

____

____________________, Secretary

resource
C

CHARITABLE CHOICE: FREQUENTLY ASKED QUESTIONS

Stanley W. Carlson-Thies

1. How do I apply for Charitable Choice money?

There is no special Charitable Choice fund for religious organizations. Charitable Choice isn't a program to aid religion, but rather a set of rules to remove legal barriers that kept many organizations with a distinct religious character from being able to compete for government funds to provide services. Charitable Choice applies when state and local governments use federal money to buy welfare services, some services for low-income families and neighborhoods (through Community Action Agencies), and some drug treatment services. Once officials have decided to buy the services, Charitable Choice requires them to allow faith-based groups to compete to win the contracts or grants to provide those services. Charitable Choice gives no special favor to religious providers, and it also doesn't box them into only offering certain services: when the money involved is covered by Charitable Choice, then faith-based groups have the same right to compete for contracts and grants that any other provider has.

2. Officials I talk to don't know anything about Charitable Choice. What should I do?

Unfortunately, too many officials haven't paid attention to the new Charitable Choice rules that they are supposed to be putting into effect. You might need to be the person who helps these officials learn what it is they should be doing. Use resources like "Charitable Choice 101: An Introduction" (www.cpjustice.org/stories/storyReader$319, reprinted in Exhibit 6.2) and "A Guide to Charitable Choice" (www.cpjustice.org/charitablechoice/guide). However, new information may not be enough: the officials' hands may be tied because officials above them or the legislature have not made the legal and regulatory changes required before funding decisions can be made according to the new rules. You and others may have to engage in some political action, contacting your elected state representatives or the governor's office and asking for the equal opportunity Charitable Choice promises. Use the Charitable Choice Petition (downloads.weblogger.com/gems/cpj/Charitable%20Choice%20Petition.pdf). For more information, see "What to Do If Officials Ignore Charitable Choice" (www.cpjustice.org/stories/storyReader$314, reprinted in Exhibit 6.5).

3. Our program offers prayer and scriptural teaching along with secular help. Is that OK under Charitable Choice?

Religious activities are protected under the U.S. Constitution and, as the public and many officials acknowledge, programs of help with a religious dimension may be just what some people in crisis need. When the government is involved, care is needed about how religious activities are offered. Charitable Choice says that religious activities (worship and prayer, instruction in religion and Bible studies, evangelism, and discipleship training) have to be voluntary and cannot be funded by government. That protects the religious liberty of people who need help, and it protects government from unconstitutionally endorsing a faith. At the same time, Charitable Choice affirms that organizations with an obvious religious character can be funded by government to provide services, it accepts that services can deal with issues of morality and values, and it permits staff to talk about spiritual matters when recipients desire it and the discussion is not held during the time of the funded service of job training, counseling, etc.

4. Doesn't Charitable Choice require the government to fund discrimination?

Charitable Choice forbids providers from discriminating against recipients on the basis of their religion or lack of faith. However, it does permit faith-based organizations to hire only employees who will adhere to the organization's religious basis and standards. Without that freedom, some organizations are unable to maintain a distinct religious atmosphere and to provide services in a faith-based way—just as a Democratic senator could hardly run an effective office without being able to exclude otherwise qualified Republican employees. Under Charitable Choice the organizations cannot discriminate arbitrarily in hiring—they have to abide by the other nondiscrimination requirements (race, age, gender, handicap, etc.). The Civil Rights Act of 1964 recognized the importance of this employment right by exempting religious organizations from the general ban on using religious criteria in hiring. Courts up to the Supreme Court have acknowledged the legitimacy and importance of this right. So Charitable Choice just says that organizations do not have to give up their preexisting religious hiring right when they receive government funding to provide social services. Government is not funding employment discrimination; the government is simply buying services from the best providers, some of which are religious organizations that have every right under preexisting law to hire only people who agree with the organization's mission and standards. For further information, see "Isn't Charitable Choice Government-Funded Discrimination?" (www.cpjustice.org/stories/storyreader$375).

5. Isn't it unconstitutional to force religion on poor and vulnerable people?

It is! Under the U.S. Constitution, the poor and vulnerable have the same right of religious liberty as everyone else. Charitable Choice honors that right with three explicit requirements: providers cannot discriminate against recipients on the basis of their religion or lack of religion; providers cannot force recipients to take part in religious activities such as prayer or Bible study; and the government must be prepared to offer a secular alternative if a recipient does not want to receive services from a religious provider. And Charitable Choice honors religious liberty in a positive sense, too. By removing barriers to the participation of religious service providers, it enlarges the variety of services that government can fund, making it more likely that people who prefer to be served by a faith-based organization can get such help.

6. Won't Charitable Choice make religion dependent on government?

Charitable Choice levels the playing field so that faith-based organizations, if they choose to, can compete for government funds to provide social services. It does not obligate any religious group to collaborate with government at all, much less contract to deliver services. If a faith-based organization does accept government funding, then it should take care not to become dependent on government—and it should take care not to become detached from the faith community that gave it birth. Taking too much money from any one source (government, a foundation, a corporate donor, or just a rich benefactor) makes any organization vulnerable. It is better to seek funds from a variety of sources and to plan in advance what to do if a major source dries up or later adds unacceptable strings to the money. At the same time, organizations have to be careful to nurture their ties with their original backers and supporters, who provide priceless guidance, enthusiasm, volunteers, and spiritual direction. Be careful so that no one begins to think that success in getting government funds means that the organization no longer values people who can contribute a few dollars, prayer, volunteer hours, and their wisdom. Beyond that, Charitable Choice is designed to enable government and faith-based groups to become allies in serving the needy, not to make religious providers mere arms of government. Both government and the religious groups should expect that, beyond providing contracted services, a religious (or secular) provider will, if necessary, advocate against officials on behalf of clients and appeal to elected officials for changes in policies.

7. Why should taxpayers have to pay for someone else's religion?

When government officials under Charitable Choice contract with a faith-based provider for social services, officials are not "buying religion" but rather making it possible for recipients to get help from an effective provider of services. Of course, those services will be shaped by the faith of the organization, just as the services offered by a secular provider are shaped by some secular viewpoint. Government's concern, and the concern of taxpayers, is that the services be effective and that the rights of recipients be protected. Charitable Choice protects recipients and tells officials to select the most effective providers, whether secular or religious. And Charitable Choice specifies that government contracts and grants have to be used to provide the specific services government is seeking, and not be diverted to pay for worship or evangelism. It may bother some taxpayers that the government contracts with a Protestant or Jewish provider. But even without Charitable Choice, government often turns to religiously affiliated groups like the Salvation Army, Jewish Federations, Lutheran Services of America, and Catholic Charities to buy needed services. And the U.S. Supreme Court has held that taxpayers have no general right to object when officials choose one provider or another or make other decisions that some taxpayers object to on moral grounds. How could government carry out its programs if each taxpayer had an individual right to refuse to support whatever programs and purchases he or she found objectionable?

8. Isn't Charitable Choice just a fancy term for the right-wing dream of shutting down welfare and giving the poor over to churches and charities?

Charitable Choice is a set of rules to guide how governments spend social-service money, not a directive to officials to stop spending money and instead steer the poor to the local house of worship or social club. Of course, if a faith-based provider offers great services for less cost so that the government can save money, who can object? And who can object if government doesn't have to do so much in the future because religious and secular groups, using private funds, have become stronger, and families and neighbors are reaching out consistently to the needy? The best society isn't the one with the highest government welfare spending but the one that best responds to need and best prevents poverty in the first place.

9. States don't have to comply with Charitable Choice unless they want to, right?

In fact, Charitable Choice is optional for states only in the sense that, as a procurement rule, of course it does not apply if a state uses the federal funds only to fund government-operated services. States have the option of supplying the services themselves or contracting with nongovernmental providers. But if they turn to outside providers, then they must follow the Charitable Choice rules. This is a legally enforceable requirement; officials who disregard Charitable Choice when they spend federal funds to which it is attached are at risk of being taken to court. Officials don't have to be enthusiastic about collaborating with faith-based providers; the requirement is binding anyway. And officials cannot ignore Charitable Choice with the argument that they don't think that faith-based providers are sufficiently skilled or properly structured to provide government-funded services; officials have to apply the Charitable Choice rules and let the faith-based organizations try to prove their competence. Officials should not give an incompetent group government funds, but they cannot prejudge a whole class of organizations and exclude all of them from competing for funding.

10. What happens to Charitable Choice when a state's constitution says the state cannot aid religious organizations?

Charitable Choice isn't a matter of government aid to religion or religious organizations; rather, it makes it possible for the government to aid people needing help by contracting with religious as well as secular providers, so long as those providers offer effective help and follow certain rules about accountability and respect for clients. The aid given under Charitable Choice is help to the needy and poor; this is nothing like the practice in some countries of taxpayer funding of houses of worship and clergy training. Beyond that, Charitable Choice is a federal rule that accompanies federal funds, so that according to the principle of federal supremacy, state and local governments must abide by the provision when they spend the federal funds. Congress acknowledged the legitimacy of state constitutions by providing that, despite Charitable Choice, states with restrictive constitutions cannot be forced to use their own money to fund programs offered by faith-based providers. If a state constitution restricts such funding, then the state may keep state funds separate from the federal funds, spending the state funds according to the state rules and the federal funds according to Charitable Choice.

11. Isn't Charitable Choice just a political slogan? Government has always funded religious organizations.

Government collaboration with religious organizations, including funding, has always been a distinctive characteristic of the American social safety net. However, in principle, government only funded secular programs offered by organizations without a marked religious character—the organizations were supposed to be "religiously affiliated" and not "pervasively sectarian." Practice has always been more flexible than theory, and laws have been inconsistent, some permitting flexible relations and others rigidly excluding religion. Charitable Choice is designed, in the first place, to give a firm foundation in law for flexible collaboration and to set a common standard for such collaboration, thus validating existing positive practices. But it also bursts real barriers that have existed in many laws. In fact, Charitable Choice was originally drafted as an antidote to unnecessary and unconstitutional restrictions in a variety of federal and state laws. Charitable Choice says that faith-based providers can display icons, organize their governing board as they choose, and hire on the basis of faith—because other laws specifically require contractors to give up some or all of these practices. What's new with Charitable Choice is not government contracting with religious organizations but rather the conditions under which it contracts. For more information, go to "Charitable Choice: Implementation" (www.cpjustice.org/charitablechoice/implementation).

Source: Used by permission of Stanley W. Carlson-Thies and the Center for Public Justice.

resource
D

GOVERNMENT FUNDING POLICY

CityTeam Ministries

I. PREAMBLE

Even though, historically, CityTeam has been closed to the idea of receiving government money, changes at the government level as well as changes in our programs make it now an exciting opportunity, but not without its risks.

It is the purpose of this policy to serve as a guide to ensure that we maximize this opportunity while minimizing the great risks associated with government funding. In addition, this policy needs to be rooted in Scripture, in harmony with our Mission Statement and closely connected with our hedgehog concept.

Our traditional opposition to government funding has been based on the conviction that we, as a Christian organization, will not compromise on the message of the Gospel. We at CityTeam firmly believe that the problems affecting the poor have a spiritual root and that only the liberating Gospel of Jesus Christ can effectively transform people. To compromise our message for the sake of receiving some funding would be the spiritual death of our ministry.

However, recent changes at the government level, in particular with the Faith-Based Initiative, are now making it possible for Christian organizations to compete for government funding without compromising on their Christian message as long as these funds are not used directly in their religious teachings but in meeting the physical needs of people.

At the same time, CityTeam has been going through major shifts over the past decade:

- From an institutionalized way of doing ministry to a relationship-based one
- From chapels and large centralized events to small community groups
- From emphasis on law to balance of grace
- From compulsory to voluntary participation
- From professionals doing ministry to "clients" doing ministry
- From doing ministry to equipping others to do ministry
- From "hit and run" evangelism to in-depth discipleship
- From handing off to others the people we lead to the Lord to establishing new communities of faith

We can summarize these changes by saying that our delivery system for the transmission of the Gospel has changed from program-based to relationship-based. These changes are certainly favorable to the possibilities of receiving government funding.

Nevertheless, there are still real risks for CityTeam with regard to government funding, among them the following:

- An unhealthy dependence on government funding
- Loss of focus on our real mission
- Loss of our Christian identity
- Loss of our strategic role

The policy will help us in establishing mechanisms to protect ourselves as much as possible from these risks.

II. BIBLICAL FOUNDATION

As we consider using government funds, and in light of the lessons we have learned from Christian organizations that have drifted as they have "followed the money," let us consider these warnings against the lure of riches and money:

"No one can serve two masters. Either he will hate the one and love the other, or he will be devoted to the one and despise the other. You cannot serve both God and Money." (Matt. 6:24)

"People who want to get rich fall into temptation and a trap and into many foolish and harmful desires that plunge men into ruin and destruction.

For the love of money is a root of all kinds of evil. Some people, eager for money, have wandered from the faith and pierced themselves with many griefs." (1 Tim. 6:9–10)

"Keep your lives free from the love of money and be content with what you have, because God has said, 'Never will I leave you; never will I forsake you.'" (Heb. 13:5)

"Whoever trusts in his riches will fall, but the righteous will thrive like a green leaf." (Prov. 11:28)

"Keep falsehood and lies far from me; give me neither poverty nor riches, but give me only my daily bread. Otherwise, I may have too much and disown you and say, 'Who is the Lord?' Or I may become poor and steal, and so dishonor the name of my God." (Prov. 30:8–9)

On the positive side, we find Biblical examples of government resources being used to further the kingdom of God:

- Pharaoh provided land and food in Egypt for Jacob and his descendants. (Gen. 47:11–12)
- King Artaxerxes provided timber to Nehemiah for the restoration of Jerusalem's walls. (Neh. 2:8)
- King David provided all kinds of resources—gold, silver, bronze, iron, and wood—for the building of the Temple in Jerusalem. (1 Chron. 29:2–3)

As we consider using government funding, we must make sure the projects or programs being supported are in harmony with our Mission Statement and our "hedgehog concept."

Mission Statement
To glorify God by serving people in need, proclaiming the Gospel, and establishing disciples among the disadvantaged people of cities.

Hedgehog Concept

We will excel at catalyzing Christ-centered discipleship movements among the poor and disadvantaged.

To protect the integrity of the ministry, we must consider the following questions:

- Does the program being funded help us accomplish our mission statement?
- Will accepting these funds create a dependence on government?
- Are we violating any Scriptural principles?
- How will these funds help us catalyze discipleship movements?

Finally, let us be mindful that though policies are helpful, they cannot fully protect us from going astray. Organizations go astray because their leaders' hearts have gone astray. We still need to rely on our Sovereign Lord to guard our ministry from spiritual corruption, and above all we must guard our hearts by following more passionately than ever the Great Commandment and the Great Commission. The life and words of a man who specialized in catalyzing discipleship movements, the Apostle Paul, are a good admonition for us:

> "Keep watch over yourselves and all the flock of which the Holy Spirit has made you overseers. Be shepherds of the church of God, which he bought with his own blood. I know that after I leave, savage wolves will come in among you and will not spare the flock. Even from your own number men will arise and distort the truth in order to draw away disciples after them. So be on your guard! Remember that for three years I never stopped warning each of you night and day with tears.
>
> Now I commit you to God and to the word of his grace, which can build you up and give you an inheritance among all those who are sanctified.
>
> I have not coveted anyone's silver or gold or clothing. You yourselves know that these hands of mine have supplied my own needs and the needs of my companions. In everything I did, I showed you that by this kind of hard work we must help the weak, remembering the words the Lord Jesus himself said: 'It is more blessed to give than to receive.'" (Acts 20:28–35)

III. POLICY STATEMENT

1. CityTeam will use government funding only for stated nonreligious program components. With funds from other sources, CityTeam will utilize the opportunities provided by the government-funded programs to fulfill its mission of serving the poor and planting churches. A written strategy and plan for this program opportunity must be completed and approved prior to submission of the grant.

2. CityTeam will accept government money (or partner with other organizations who do so) only if a "cause-and-effect" strategy of connection to CityTeam's core business of church planting is clearly articulated in writing. This arrangement must also include a person responsible to implement that strategy, clearly stated progress benchmarks, and a mechanism for reporting to the president.

3. CityTeam will accept government money only if there is a clear written plan for sustainability or a written exit strategy that includes all of the following elements:

- The source of funding to sustain the project when the government funds are exhausted
- The plan for termination of the project, service, or program when the government grant has been consumed.
- The termination, reassignment, or alternative source of funding for any people compensated with funds from the government grant.
- The process of evaluating the project and a plan to return the money and abandon the project if the strategy for connecting to church planting proves not to be viable.

4. CityTeam will accept government money only if the government-stipulated purpose for the use of the money aligns with CityTeam's core business of service to the poor.

5. CityTeam will not accept any government money if accommodating the restrictions of the government grant would cause CityTeam to compromise its doctrinal statement or core values or in any way restrict or jeopardize any of its rights and privileges as a religious nonprofit now or in the future.

6. CityTeam will not launch any project or program based solely on the expectation of future government funding.

IV. PROCEDURES

1. An oversight committee (Government Funding Committee) will be established to monitor CityTeam's involvement with government funding. This committee will include the CFO or designee, VP of Fund Development or designee, and a city director.

2. Prior to submission of any application, the applicant (CityTeam department or project) must receive authorization to apply from the Government Funding Committee. This "request for authorization to apply" shall be the responsibility of the city director and must include the government department being targeted, the anticipated amount, the life span of the grant, the sustainability plan or exit plan, the impact the funding will have on the operation of the ministry, and the key contact person responsible for the project. Primary to this request is a definition of how the project being funded is connected to CityTeam's core business of church planting. The president or CFO may grant exceptions to the timing of the items included in the government grant application process (a template will be developed for this process).

3. All grant applications must be signed by the CFO or designee prior to submission.

4. The following persons or groups shall be authorized to accept government funds on behalf of CityTeam:

- Up to $100,000: Government Funding Committee
- $100,001 to $1,999,999: Government Funding Committee, National Executive Team
- Over $2,000,000: Government Funding Committee, National Executive Team, Trustees Executive Committee

5. The city director will be responsible to monitor and ensure proper reporting of projects that use government funds:

- To ensure compliance with finance department procedures
- To ensure that the stated outcomes of the project are achieved
- To ensure that CityTeam ministry objectives are being accomplished
- To ensure compliance with the stated sustainability plan or exit strategy
- To ensure that required government reporting is completed

6. All reports to the funding source as stipulated by the source shall be completed by the city director and will be submitted by the Finance Department. The Finance Department will be responsible for compliance with the required reporting timetables.

7. The Human Resource Department shall notify all staff hired using government funds, in writing and at the time of hiring, that CityTeam intends to use the project to create opportunities for evangelism and church planting. The program to which their specific role is connected shall also be made clear to them: either the government-funded project or the program designed to use the opportunity for CityTeam's core ministry that is afforded by the government-funded project.

8. Staff hired into programs funded by government money shall be trained and sign acknowledgments of training related to the relationship of the government-funded projects and the core ministry programs that are designed using the opportunity afforded by the government-funded project. This training shall be the responsibility of the city director.

Source: Reprinted with the permission of CityTeam.

resource

E

WHERE TO GO FOR HELP

WEB SITES

Center for Public Justice: www.cpjuctice.org

Publishes most research and government guidelines for public awareness.

We Care America: www.wecareamerica.org

Conducts training sessions in grantwriting, capacity building, and public policy through federal partnerships.

Hudson Institute: www.hudson.org

Washington, D.C., think tank performing research and publishing work by respected experts such as Amy Sherman, researcher and author, Hudson Institute; Ryan Streeter, author and director of the Office of Faith-Based and Community Initiatives at the U.S. Department of Housing and Urban Development; John DiIulio, former director of the White House Office of Faith-Based and Community Initiatives.

Alban Institute: www.alban.org

Publisher and consultant service for mainline denominations and congregations.

Christian Community Development Association: www.ccda.org

Serves churches involved in community development and related matters.

Corporation for National and Community Service: www.nationalservice.org

A federal volunteer mobilization agency.

Brand in the Box: www.brandinthebox.com

An Internet marketing company for nonprofits.

Foundation Center: www.fdncenter.org

Helps in all aspects of nonprofit work.

GuideStar: www.guidestar.org

Lists 990 tax forms and general giving information on over 800,000 nonprofits.

Center for Law and Religious Freedom/Christian Legal Society: www.clsnet.org

Has lawyers and legal professionals familiar with common problems in the field of faith-based social ministry.

Alliance Defense Fund: www.adf.org

Known for taking on tough social legal battles concerning matters of faith.

GOVERNMENT RESOURCES

White House Office of Faith-Based and Community Initiatives

The White House

Washington, DC 20502

www.fbcs.gov

U.S. Department of Justice

Patrick Purtill, Director

950 Pennsylvania Avenue, NW

Washington, DC 20530

www.ojp.usdoj.gov/fbci

U.S. Department of Labor
Brent Orrell, Director
200 Constitution Avenue, NW
Washington, DC 20210
www.dol.gov/cfbci

U.S. Department of Health and Human Services
Bobby Polito, Director
200 Independence Avenue, SW
Washington, DC 20201
www.hhs.gov/fbci

U.S. Department of Housing and Urban Development
Steven Wagner, Director
451 Seventh Street SW
Washington, DC 20410
www.hud.gov/offices/fbci

U.S. Department of Education
John Porter, Director
555 New Jersey Avenue, NW
Washington, DC 20208
www.ed.gov/faithandcommunity

U.S. Department of Agriculture
Juliet McCarthy, Director
Fourteenth and Independence Avenues, SW
Washington, DC 20250
www.usaid.gov

CONSULTANTS

Alford Group: www.alford.com

Has offices throughout the United States specializing in nonprofit management, fundraising strategies, capital campaigns, and related matters.

Alban Institute: www.alban.org

Offers a variety of consultants who travel and conduct training sessions for churches and smaller nonprofits involved in social ministry.

Community Colleges

Visit your local community college Web site's business department or nonprofit listings, and contact the instructors for leads on local consultants.

PUBLICATIONS FROM THE CENTER FOR PUBLIC JUSTICE

Accountability Guidelines for Government and Social Ministries, by Clark Cochran (1998)

Are Faith-Based Programs More Effective? by Stephen V. Monsma (2000)

Charitable Choice for Welfare Community Services, by Stanley W. Carlson-Thies (2000)

The Charitable Choice Handbook for Ministry Leaders, by Amy L. Sherman (2001)

Fruitful Collaboration Between Government and Christian Social Ministries, by Amy L. Sherman (1998)

Government Cooperation with Social Ministries, by Stephen V. Monsma (1998).

The Growing Impact of Charitable Choice, by Amy L. Sherman (2000)

Isn't Charitable Choice Government Funded Discrimination? by Carl H. Esbeck (2001)

Payne Memorial Outreach and Charitable Choice, by Stephen Lazarus and Molly Marsh (2001)

Project Heritage and Charitable Choice, by Randall L. Frame (2000)

The Regulation of Religious Organizations as Recipients of Governmental Assistance, by Carl H. Esbeck (1996)

Welfare Responsibility of Government and Churches, by Luis E. Lugo (1998)

We're All "Faith-Based" Now, by Stephen Lazarus (2001)

OTHER PUBLICATIONS

Collaboration: What Makes It Work, by Paul Mattessich, Marta Murray-Close, Barbara Monsey, and the Wilder Research Center (St. Paul, Minn.: Amherst H. Wilder Foundation, 2001)

Compassionate Conservatism, by Marvin Olasky (New York: Free Press, 2000)

Developing an Evaluation Component for Your Proposal, by Jane Arsensault (Providence, R.I.: Support Center, 1994)

God, Government, and the Good Samaritan, by Joseph Loconte (Washington, D.C.: Heritage Foundation, 2001)

Improving Nonprofit Boards, by Mary Stewart Hall (Seattle, Wash.: Seattle University, 2000)

Myths, Miscues, and Misconceptions: No-Aid Separationism and the Establishment Clause, by Carl H. Esbeck (Notre Dame, Ind.: Notre Dame Law School, 1999)

Partnership Quotient Self-Assessment, by Arthur Himmelman (Minneapolis, Minn.: Himmelman Consulting, 2001)

Rallying the Armies of Compassion, by George W. Bush (Washington, D.C.: Government Printing Office, 2001)

A Revolution of Compassion: Faith-Based Groups as Full Partners in Fighting America's Social Problems, by Dave Donaldson and Stanley W. Carlson-Thies (Grand Rapids, Mich.: Baker Books, 2003)

The Scattered Voice, by James W. Skillen (Grand Rapids, Mich.: Zondervan, 1990)

Welfare in America, edited by Stanley W. Carlson-Thies and James W. Skillen (Grand Rapids, Mich.: Eerdmans, 1996)

INDEX

F

G

Q

R

S

T

U

V

W